Magic Child is the story of a crooked journey from childhood to womanhood. The reader becomes aware bit by bit— through little Kit's imaginary friend, through older Kit's repeated accidents and warped relationships—that something is very wrong.

This is one woman's journey of discovery, pain and recovery. With grippingly honest prose, Basom tackles big themes—the reflection of societal oppression in personal lives, the warping effects of pain, the elusiveness of memory, the persistence of hope, the occasionally and unaccountably miraculous effect of tragedy. Despite its portrayal of twisted morality, abuse and anger, the book falls neither into blame, hopelessness nor simplistic optimism. This is a movingly and artfully written personal saga and an inspiring one, suffused with a warm playful spirit.

Kit Basom is a powerful new arrival in print. She is American of Scots ancestry presently living in a cabin in the Rocky Mountains. She dances, makes gingerbread trees and works as a maid, a body worker and critic. Her patchwork career has included training teachers of American Indian students; consulting for the National Geographic Society; dance instruction; science education; coaching rowing and pumping gas. She has spent most of the last nine years in arid Colorado "walking on the bones of the earth" and is now feeling drawn by the fleshier deciduous forest.

For the Magic Child in you, Patricia

magic child

warmly from Kit

Kit Basom

Argyll publishing

First published in 1992 by
Argyll Publishing
Glendaruel
Argyll
PA22 3AE

Acknowledgements are due to Press Gang Publishers, Vancouver, B.C. for permission to quote from *Daughters of Copper Woman*

British Library Cataloguing-in-Publication Data.
A catalogue record for this book is available from the British Library.

ISBN 1 874640 15 7

Cover painting by Diane Watson *Isis II*
Cover design by Marcia Clark
Typset by W McLean, Dunoon
Linotronic output by Cordfall, Civic Street, Glasgow
Printed and bound in Great Britain by The Cromwell Press, Broughton Gifford, Melksham, Wiltshire

For my mother and father
in their anguish and their love.

Face the monster until it gives you a gift.

Acknowledgements

I thank Georgia and Greg, the two people most responsible for creating enough safety for my story to emerge again from the darkness where it had been kept most of my life.

I thank the people whose own stories loosened my buried memories: Michael WhirlwindSoldier, Amos, Paul, Mary, Joseph, Chris Bordeaux, Howard BadHand, Ozzie Williamson, John, Patrick Wilmot and Jack Fry. I thank the other American Indian people I have come to know and who helped me see my own culture, my family and myself from a new and freeing perspective.

I thank Ellie Bemis for emotional, financial and spiritual support. I thank Dave Merritt and Sarah Hill for their sturdy friendship.

This book was born while I was travelling. Like any other pregnancy, this one had its own schedule and the baby did not ask if this would be a convenient time for it to arrive. So delivery occurred while I was without a home and on the move, something like having a baby on a cross-town bus. I thank the people who allowed me to stay in their spare rooms, uncommunicative and distant as the birth took place: especially Graham Noble, my parents and Dave Merritt. I thank Dave also for helping me make friends with a computer so I could prepare the manuscript for publication and for helping me through the times when I was not on such friendly terms with the machine. I thank my brother Nash for providing the computer to befriend and Richard and Cheri Skurdall for loaning me another while I was on the road in Vermont.

I thank my agent Cathie Thomson and publisher Derek Rodger for their faith in the work, despite the fact that the first copy either of them saw was a pile of hand-written, cut-and-pasted pages in a paper bag.

I thank my family—my parents Ruth and Bill Basom, my brothers Nash, Scott and Ken Basom, my Aunt Helen and my cousins Miriam Rose, Carol and Henry—for their support and courage as I uncovered hidden bits of all our pasts and then made the decision to publish this story, which is also theirs.

Kit Basom
Nederland, Colorado
September 1992

Author's Note

The substance of this book comes from my own memory. The names of some people have been changed or omitted to protect their privacy. In a few instances, events were consolidated to allow for smoother narration. Otherwise the story recounted here is true to the best of my knowledge and recollection.

Reference is made in the text to certain items that may be unfamiliar to British readers. For those who are curious, I include the following notes about some of these American objects, phenomena, places and events.

A *sweat lodge* is a type of small hut used by many North American Indians for cleansing ceremonies. The word "sweat" is used as a verb and as a noun referring to the ceremony itself. The ceremonies take different forms but always include the element of intense heat created by placing hot stones in the centre of the lodge.

The *Sun Dance* is a four-day gathering of Sioux people. Some of the participants have wooden skewers inserted under the skin of their chests, leaving both ends of the skewers exposed (like straight pins through fabric). Leather thongs which are attached at one end to the top of a tall pole are then tied to the ends of the skewers. At one point in the ceremony the dancers lean back, suspending their weights from the bites of their chests until the flesh tears. Chris participated in this and other parts of the Sun Dance.

The *Navajo Reservation,* covering 16 million acres of Arizona,

New Mexico and Utah, is the largest Indian reservation in the U.S. The Navajos are also the largest tribal group in the country. Because of the scale of geography and population, the Navajos are able to maintain a higher degree of autonomy and traditional culture than many other North American tribes.

A *Yeibichai* is a several-day, Navajo, healing ceremony, which can be held during the winter. It is for the purpose of restoring a person to harmony with the universe. Inside a hogan, a medicine person makes sand paintings on the dirt floor and repeats a ritual pattern of movement and song all night long.

A *hogan* is the traditional round or many-sided home of the Navajos. It may be made of any material (logs, lumber, stone, branches and mud, cinder blocks) and consists of one unpartitioned room.

A *petroglyph* is a design pecked into the surface of a large stone. Tens of thousands of these ancient designs exist in the canyon country of southern Utah and throughout the North American desert Southwest.

Slickrock is the smooth sandstone characteristic of Utah's canyon country.

Contents

I Inside Time: Safety for the Journey (1985, Kit) 19

II Before Remembering: Lost in the Forest (1953-1984, Toby) 29

1. Knock-Out
2. Swinging
3. The Twist of the Ribbon
4. Jail
5. Magic Trees
6. Permanent
7. All Straightened Out
8. Cancer
9. Out for a Pass
10. Bloody Rags
11. Horse
12. The Roof
13. Sledding
14. Better Than a Pillow
15. A Hole in the Wall
16. Something Weird
17. Waterfall
18. Iracles

19. Onions
20. Trapdoor
21. Break-In
22. The Smoker Who Doesn't Smoke
23. Thick, Heavy, and Sharp
24. Pierced Ears
25. Soft Mommy
26. Trapdoor
27. Abai
28. The Man, the Cop, and the Back
29. No Expectations
30. Shocked
31. Trapdoor
32. The Man, the Cop, and the Back—Again

III Getting Ready to Remember: Bear Tracks 77
(1984-1987, Kit)

1. The Beast
2. The Confession
3. Bear Claws
4. Dowsing Rods
5. Death and Children
6. Journeys
7. The Mouse
8. Hummingbirds
9. Fawns
10. The Wind Rivers
11. Paul
12. Grizzly
13. Neighbors
14. Michael WhirlwindSoldier
15. Magic Children
16. Haunted Hotel

17. Al and Howard
18. The Rain on the Plane
19. Ozzie
20. Before Dinner or After?

IV Before Forgetting: Losing Her Way 159
(1949-1952, Toby)

V After Remembering: Walking in the Woods 167
(1987-1990, Toby)

1. Toby and the Flappy Man
2. Another Bear
3. Another Trapdoor
4. Thick, Heavy, and Sharp
5. The Rotten Orange and the Map
6. The Sliding Board
7. The Cocoon
8. More Magic Trees
9. Nuts aren't Hummingbirds
10. Walls
11. Another Knock-Out
12. Prayer Sticks
13. Sharks' Teeth
14. Maya Angelou
15. Slippery Memories
16. The Red Fish
17. Cornered by Another Good Man
18. The Body Knows
19. The Letter
20. An Open Hand
21. Summer and You're Packing
22. Bread and Puppet
23. Money

24. Wet Suit
25. Surgery

VI Outside Time: Desert Heart (1990, Kit) 255

Part I

INSIDE TIME: SAFETY FOR THE JOURNEY
(1985, Kit)

Time and again the magic did not do what was needed and so the council gathered and told them that, when this happened, it did not mean the magic was gone, nor did it mean the Old Ones were angry, it meant simply that it was Time. Time for movement.

From the mythic tradition
of the native women of Vancouver Island
as related by
Anne Cameron in *Daughters of Copper Woman*

"How many stones?"

"I don't know. I should have noticed. What an obvious thing to have noticed, how many stones, and how silly that I didn't."

"So, how long were you in the sweat lodge?"

I was asked to tell about the ceremony I attended at an Indian reservation in Minnesota. But I don't know the answers to these questions. I flirt with embarrassment, even shame, and then decide against these in favor of fascination. Yes, what obvious things to have noticed, and how *interesting* that I didn't. I start to tell what I do remember, while taking pleasure now in noticing what I don't, for it's these gaps which illuminate the specialness of this event in my life. Almost wholly discontinuous with my previous experience, this afternoon in the tiny, dark lodge offered no familiar landmarks by which I could orient my senses.

We crawled into the low lodge, moving sunwise (which I took to mean clockwise), women first. The teenager who was the only other female in the group pushed me in front of her, so I led. I don't know what covered the dirt floor, if anything. Maybe towels, maybe cut grass, maybe nothing. My mind was searching for information of another sort: how to behave properly in this unfamiliar setting, how to avoid offending our hosts, and how perhaps to be enriched by the experience if I could only tame my nervousness about these questions of etiquette.

As instructed, I crawled nearly all the way around the lodge and sat, leaving room for one person between me and the door to my left. The men came in. Well, when I looked they were there. We formed a single ring, our backs curved against the curving stick walls. Amos, the man who had offered us the sweat for safety on our canoe trip down the Mississippi, sat next to me, his assistant Chris on the other side of the doorway. The lodge was crowded. Our folded legs lapped over each other's. Our shoulders touched.

My fear was building. The August afternoon was already scorching. I was already a little queasy with the heat. I'm afraid of heat. I close down and tighten around it. What was I doing in a tiny, cramped hut where, I imagined, I was about to be baked like a loaf of bread?

A boy, a teenager, responding to Amos's request, tilted a shovel into the doorway, allowing a surprisingly hot stone to roll onto the ground. Amos picked it up with a pair of antlers and placed it in the pit just inches from all our knees, which were suddenly even more overlapped in reaction to the intense heat. He chanted each stone into place. There might have been four or five or six. Cardinal directions, maybe earth and sky as well. But I'm making that up. I don't remember, never knew.

Amos is the spiritual leader of the group of people who live on the Prairie Island Indian Reservation. His grey hair, which had been tied back when I met him, was now loose around his shoulders. Although small in stature, Amos seemed huge. His presence seemed to extend for several feet beyond the limit of his body, making him so big that I felt I was inside him as I sat next to him. That felt fine.

I was going to die. There was no air. The flaps were thrown over the small doorway. But Amos had said, "Whenever you're finished, just tell me and you can leave. We don't all have to finish at the same time." How gently he had put that. It was clear what this sweat was not. It wasn't a test or a contest or a requirement or a performance which would be ruined by someone's leaving. It was a gift, the best thing he had, and he was giving it to us. "You don't have to leave behind your beliefs or your doubts to come into the sweat lodge," he had assured us. "That's what you take with you. You can get whatever you want from the sweat."

It was completely dark, airless, hot. My eyes did not adjust. There was no light to come into my frantically dilated pupils. My lungs searched for air that wasn't there, clawing at the low ceiling for a breath. Panic tickled my rib cage.

Then my heart started pounding in a deep, strange rhythm. This was panic, solid and true. I would die or, skipping death entirely, look directly into God's face. God's face? Out of what deep well into my childhood did that phrase surface? The concept of God had long since dropped from my thinking.

But suddenly it was all irrelevant. Even the heat was irrelevant now, or it was just heat, no longer frightening. And, somehow, there was air. And sweat, like ants, streamed down my scalp and sides and stomach. And my heart continued to beat wildly against my ribs. Like a drum. No, it *was* a drum. There was a drum in the lodge. A big one, I guessed, from the deep resonance of it, so deep that for minutes or a minute or a thousand years I thought it was my heart inside me.

But this might not have been when it actually happened, for there were cycles during the ceremony. The chanting—oh, did I mention there was chanting?—would stop and the flaps would be lifted. (This happened more than twice, fewer than ten times.) Light and air transformed the lodge. A bucket of water was brought in. Amos kept the bucket and passed the dripping dipper to the left. Chris drank. The man next to him drank. Perhaps there was a drop for the third man. I didn't notice. The dipper would be empty long before it reached me. But my thirsty eyes peered into it just to make sure, before I passed it to Amos. He dipped it again and, again, passed it to Chris, who drank. "Well, I hadn't actually expected there to be water to drink, so I can't be disappointed," I tried to convince myself. The empty dipper passed through my hands once more and was refilled and given again to Chris, who, I now noticed, had a drum. The dipper went around and around. Do you suppose...? My rigid denial of disappointment began to sway, like a stiff grass in a stiffer wind. One by one, those early in the circle began to pass the dipper on without drinking, leaving water for the others. Amos continued to pass the dipper until, at last, it returned to him with water in it. How simple. Our thirst was quenched. More stones were rolled in. The whole sequence happened each time the flaps were opened. The stones' arrival seemed no longer dangerous, just hot. The flaps closed and a new cycle began.

Suddenly my nostrils were all that existed and they were on fire. Or were they smelling something? A flexing of Amos's shoulder muscles against mine made me aware that his right arm had moved away from his body. He was throwing something onto the furnace of stones—sage, I think—which, I felt sure, vaporized, burned, and went straight up my nose before it hit the stones. Good and bad seemed suddenly meaningless. The sharp sensation in my nostrils was all.

Then a boy said he was ready to leave. Or, actually, the older man next to him said, "This one's had enough." The flaps were opened and he crawled or we passed him across our legs to Amos and the cool afternoon. (Yes, it seemed cool in the brilliance beyond the flaps.) His leaving was OK, just as Amos had said it would be.

During one cycle, after we had drunk and more stones had been rolled in and the flaps were closed against light and air, we each had a chance to speak. Amos had told us there would be a time for this. He had encouraged us to speak in whatever language felt comfortable (there were several languages represented in the group) and to say whatever we felt. "If there are words you say at important times," Amos had told us, "if there is a prayer or a song for a special occasion, you can say it or sing it. Or you can tell us about the river or how you feel about your new friends. Whatever you want. If you want to talk to a god or the grandfathers or to us, that's fine." Chris started, chanting for, I think, several minutes in a language I didn't know.

A part of me started to slip away. No, a part of me started to arrive. I was experiencing the sweat on at least two distinct levels. I knew that Chris was finishing and that the man next to him was beginning to chant in English. "Grandfather, we sit in awe of your works as we are gathered at this beautiful spot by this mightiest of rivers. Let the spirit of the water flow into us and teach us..." He chattered on and on in a rapid sing-song. I was irritated. It was phony. He was performing. In fact, he really is a professional singer. Seemed to me he didn't know how to turn it off. But what do I know? Maybe he was completely transported. But one part of my mind heard him and thought he was phony. Then I remembered Amos's admonition that we leave behind bad feelings toward others. I let the lilting voice wash over me. And on another level, I entered a world I'd have said did not exist until I found myself there.

An eagle! At the same time or bursting through a membrane from somewhere entirely outside time, it flew into the lodge and landed on my shoulders. Its talons pierced my muscles as the skewers had pierced Chris's breast at the Sun Dance. (I'd noticed the scars, two sets. How could a person do that a second time?)

Pain shot like a fiery explosion through my flesh. It was not a bad thing. As the bird spread its wings, its talons sank more deeply into my shoulders, triggering new charges of pain. Then, stepping down onto the hot stones, wings still spread, it turned slowly around, sunwise, to face each person. It seemed—but I don't use this word—like a blessing. So, it was a gesture of blessing. The eagle flew back into the darkness beyond time.

Drained, exalted, crying, I listened to a man talking simply about the Mississippi River and the people he had met there. "I am coming from another place and you are kind to me. I thank you that you are my friends." Although German, he chose to speak in English, I suppose because it was we, not a god or a German, he wished to address.

A robed woman stepped in front of me. How could I see her in the total darkness? And how could she stand on the hot stones? She knelt facing me, her knees touching my shins. I couldn't see her face as it was shaded by her hood. Unflinching, she thrust her bare arms into my chest and pulled out my heart. Terror shot its electric tentacles through me. My mouth, my eyes, my chest all gaped. I sat shocked, my insides exposed to the fierce, calm woman whose arms dripped my blood. But somehow I knew that her hands were a good place for my heart to be. She stood and walked out of the sweat lodge, taking my heart with her.

The girl to my right had just finished her prayer. The realization that I was now supposed to speak shocked me suddenly and completely into the thin reality of darkness surrounding a circle of people in a small lodge. I had not thought of something to say. Because I sat next-to-last in the circle of which Chris was first, the dipper's sunwise movement had worried me and made me aware of my thirst. The identical circling of the talking had given me hope that I'd have time to think of something profound to say.

The silence expanded.

"Grandfather," I began, because everyone else had started that way, "although I don't know what they mean, thank you for the eagle who pierced my shoulders with its talons and for the woman who took my heart."

I was acutely aware of the close circle of people, close now in many ways. Amos asked if I was finished. I must have said yes. He chanted. Then for the third or tenth time the flaps were lifted. We crawled sunwise over the mats or ponchos or dirt into the tear-refracted sunshine and threw buckets of cold water over each other.

Amos came and sat next to me on a log. We didn't say much.

Part II

BEFORE REMEMBERING: LOST IN THE FOREST

(1953-1984, Toby)

I would like to turn over
but which side is the bed on?

1. Knock-Out

She's a knock-out. I heard a man at church say that about Kit, and I know why. When her big brothers were at school she found this tall, skinny mattress box in their room. Her brothers were getting big, so they needed bigger beds. Anyway, this big box was real neat. It was standing on its end next to the chest of drawers. Kit climbed onto the dresser and jumped into the box. That seemed like a good idea. But when she got inside, it wasn't really any fun 'cause she couldn't move. But she was so little—only about four years old—she couldn't get out. So, she leaned forward and it fell over. Her arms tried to jump up in front of her so she wouldn't hurt herself when she hit the floor, but the box was too skinny so they got stuck down low. Kit's face hit the floor real hard.

When she opened her eyes, she saw her mommy's face. Then she felt blankets and she knew she was in bed even though it was daytime. Kit got sick after that and the doctor told her mommy not to let her go to sleep even though she was real tired.

2. Swinging

The swing made a squeaking noise when it went forward but it didn't squeak when it went back. Kit decided to remember that. She also noticed the smell of the dust that her brown Oxfords brought up as they scraped the gravel away from under the swing. That also made a crunching noise that got less crunchy the more she did it. There was the feel of the big links of the chains in her hands, too. They started cool, then they got the same as her hands, unless she moved them. Then the chain was cool again.

Kit decided to remember everything about sitting in the swing that day because she just thought of something important and she wanted to remember it. She thought maybe if she remembered the whole thing she'd have a better chance of remembering her idea.

Here's what she was thinking. (And she really did remember it, too.) "Grown-ups say they want to be kids again. I'm never gonna say that. 'Cause being a kid is not what they say. It's hard. And there are lots of problems. They musta forgotten, if they can say kids are lucky 'cause they don't have problems. I'm never gonna forget. I'm never gonna forget this ever."

3. The Twist of the Ribbon

It got dark while they were driving up to Grandpa Basom's for Thanksgiving. It wasn't Thanksgiving yet. It was the day before Thanksgiving. The whole family, which was Kit and her two big brothers and their mommy and daddy, were going to Pennsylvania for the holiday. They did that every year. Kit remembered the smell of the turkeys who lived out behind Grandpa's house. There must be a hundred of them. And they left feathers all over the place. Then there was the dark color of the pickled eggs Great Aunt Minnie made. They looked more like beets. In fact, I think they got that red color from beets. There was a long, skinny couch in the upstairs room. Kit's daddy and grandpa turned it around to face the wall. Then Kit's mommy covered the crackled, black leather with a sheet and some blankets, and that made Kit's little nest.

It was perfect for not falling out, 'cause it had an arm at each end. So, she had her own tiny room held in between the wall and the couch back and arms. Kit liked it there in her private place.

But they weren't at Grandpa and Aunt Minnie's yet. Kit's daddy said there was still a long way to go and Kit could sleep in the back of the car if she wanted. But right now she was staring out the back window at the two lines of lights. There was a line of white lights. That was the line their car was in. And there was also a line of red lights. After a while, Kit turned around to tell everyone that they were in the white line. But when she looked out the front window, she saw that they were in the red line. She turned around to check in the back. This was confusing. She checked both ways a couple times. They were definitely in the white line when she looked out back and in the red line when she looked in front. Then she noticed that the lines were on different sides of the road depending on which way you looked. Suddenly she understood. There was a giant striped ribbon on the road. With a red stripe and a white stripe. And their car was right in the twist of the ribbon. They must be the most important car. They were right in the middle.

This was a big discovery. But it was maybe too complicated to explain, so Kit lay down and went to sleep.

4. Jail

Kit was lying on the floor of the car, trying to squish under the back seat so the policemen wouldn't see her. She didn't see any policemen but she knew they were there. They're always there, like God. If you do anything bad, God and the policemen see you and take you to jail.

She knew what jail was like. There were red devils there (like the one that said bad things in Kit's head) with horns and long tails and pitchforks and it was hot 'cause there was fire all around. Bad people went there. Sometimes people said, "Go to hell," and that's what they meant. That's where the policemen take bad people and poke them with pitchforks. And in Monopoly if you land on a certain square it says, "Go to jail. Go directly to jail." Only in Monopoly it was just a game. Still, Kit was glad she was too little to play Monopoly 'cause she didn't like the part about going to hell.

So, she was squishing under the seat 'cause they were doing something wrong. Her daddy noticed something on the way up to Pennsylvania for Thanksgiving with Grandpa Basom and Aunt Minnie. He noticed that the new road was all finished except for the painted lines, but part of it was still closed. When they got to the road block on their way back to Virginia, the place where you're supposed to swerve onto the old road, he didn't do it. He went around the big sign and drove on the new road. He thought it would be fun. Kit couldn't understand why he was smiling when they were all about to be thrown in jail and get burned and poked with pitchforks. That's when she got down on the floor to hide.

She never figured out why the policemen didn't get them, 'cause you can't really hide from them. Maybe they were busy arresting other people or maybe they were feeling nice or maybe they liked her daddy 'cause he was a minister. She just didn't know.

5. Magic Trees

Nash helped build the hill with wooden blocks. And Scott helped put the snow on. It was really a roll of cotton. He also cut the hole for the lake, which was really a mirror. But then Kit wanted to do the rest by herself.

She spent a long time putting the little lead people in the scene on the windowsill. She could put them anywhere she wanted. Her mommy said so. She put some skaters on the mirror. She moved them around like they were skating. Then she put some sledders and skiers on the hill. She slid them down the cotton to the lake. Then she put them on top of the hill again and slid them down again. She had them take turns so it would be safe and they wouldn't have accidents. Then she went outside and picked some maple twigs to use as trees. They looked great once Nash figured a way to use clay under the cotton to make them stand up. Finally she had everything in a way she liked. But all through Christmas she kept coming back to the windowsill and moving the people around to make a new picture. She was allowed to do that as much as she wanted. She was God for those lead people.

While Kit was fixing the windowsill people one time, someone knocked at the door. As usual, Kit ran into the kitchen and hid in the broom closet.

"Kit, it's A.J. He has a Christmas present for you," called Bill, Kit's daddy.

Well, if it was A.J., then it would be OK to come out. He was Kit's sorta extra grandfather. Her real grandfathers lived far away, one in Canada and one in Pennsylvania. But A.J. lived just up the hill, and he did fun things with Kit. Like, one time he invited her to come rake leaves behind his house. His backyard slanted down toward the woods. And the trees grew right up next to his lawn and some of them grew *in* his lawn. In the fall, the big, thick oak leaves fell all over the grass. They were brown and smooth and smelled clean, and made a good noise when you scuffed through a bunch of them. So, it was real nice of A.J. to let Kit come help rake them. They piled the leaves on a big blanket and dragged them back into the woods. They did that a buncha times. It was loads of fun, especially jumping in the huge pile they made.

Another time Kit came home from preschool and there was

a little jar on the back stoop. It had a tiny dead snake in it in alcohol. Kit's mommy read her the note. It said, "For Kit. Love, A.J." Later he came by and told Kit that he killed the snake by mistake when he was digging in his garden. He would never kill it on purpose. But since it was dead, he didn't want to waste it. And he thought he knew someone who would like it. He was right. Kit loved the little snake and kept it with her most special things.

So, now A.J. was there with a Christmas present. Kit came outa the broom closet and went into the living room. She could hardly believe her eyes. Standing on the floor was a tree almost as tall as she was. A.J. gave her a letter that went with the tree. Actually, it was a story.

The same thing happened last Christmas, when Kit was five. A.J. brought Kit a little tree. It was a real holly tree in a bucket, and it was decorated with popcorn and cranberries. Later, when it wasn't so cold, A.J. came back and helped Kit plant the tree beside the house. She went out to check it nearly everyday. That tree came with a story, too. It was about how A.J. was walking in the forest by the Chesapeake Bay. He and his wife Janet had a log cabin on a cliff by the Bay. Sometimes Kit got to visit them there and sleep in a high, wooden bed in the downstairs room. Once Janet came and woke Kit up in the middle of the night and told her to come outside 'cause a storm was coming. Kit was upset at first about being wakened, but then she went outside and stood on the edge of the cliff with Janet and they watched the storm coming across the Bay. More and more stars went out till the sky was all black. The waves started crashing louder and louder at the bottom of the cliff. The wind started blowing Kit's pajamas tight against the fronts of her legs. When big drops of rain started flying into their faces, Janet and Kit ran back into the cabin laughing.

Nearly everyday at the Bay, Kit and A.J. went for walks.

They walked on the beach and collected sharks' teeth and shells, but mostly sharks' teeth. One time A.J. stopped for no reason and just looked out at the water. Kit was just waiting for him to start walking again. Suddenly she saw the biggest shark's tooth she ever saw. "A.J., there's a huge shark's tooth right by your toe! You practically stepped on it! But I found it!" A.J. smiled.

Other times they walked in the woods up on the cliff. The trees were different from the ones back in Kit's neighborhood. There were oaks, but they were small and different. And there were persimmons. The fruit made your mouth pucker if it wasn't ripe. Once A.J. pried open a persimmon seed so Kit could see the fork inside. Persimmon seeds always have a tiny, white spoon or fork inside. There were also holly trees. And that's what A.J. brought Kit when she was five. The story with that tree told about how he was walking through the woods by the Bay and then this little holly tree asked him to take it to Kit. So, he dug it up very carefully and put it in a bucket and he and Janet decorated it and brought it to Kit.

This year's tree was different. It had a thin, brown trunk like a broom handle and thinner branches coming out. Gingerbread people were dangling from all the branches. Kit stared and stared at the gingerbread tree. She was too shy to hug A.J.—she hardly ever hugged anyone unless she had to—but she looked at him and smiled.

When A.J. left, Kit's daddy read the story that came with the tree. It started off the same way as last year's, with A.J. walking in the forest by the Bay. But this time he got lost and ended up in a part of the woods he never saw before. Then a funny, little man, only about two-feet tall, told A.J. to follow him. The little man led him to a magic part of the forest and showed him the gingerbread tree. He told A.J. that this tree was for Kit and asked if A.J. would be willing to chop it down and take it to her. And that's what he did.

After Christmas, Kit's family ate the gingerbread people. Then they pulled the branches outa the trunk and saved the tree for next Christmas. Kit's mother said she would make gingerbread people to go on it next year. And she did.

The next year, A.J. brought another tree that was from the Bay. It was driftwood with shells and sharks' teeth hanging from it. So, that year Kit had the holly tree that was growing outside and the gingerbread tree and the shell tree inside.

By the next year, Kit was getting interested in birds. A.J. knew that, and he brought Kit a little pine tree decorated with suet and peanut-butter balls and seeds and all sorts of things she could share with the birds.

Kit began to expect A.J. to come by a few days before Christmas each year and give her a tree. She always wondered what it would be this time, and then she'd remind herself that maybe he wouldn't bring her one that year. It wasn't like he promised to give her a tree every year. But he always did bring one, until the year he died right before Christmas.

6. Permanent

Permanent. Kit knew what that meant. It would never go away. Her hair would be stuck like that for the rest of her life. She cried real loud and banged her head against the floor one more time to try to smash the curls or at least make the pain go away. Her head hurt a lot. All she could think to do was cry and hit her head against the floor. Once Kit looked up and saw her mother looking real sad. But then the pain got too strong and she started hitting her head on the floor again.

Kit knew her mother was sorry about the permanent. She would never have made Kit get it if Kit had just said she didn't want it. But Kit didn't say anything when they went to the beauty parlor to get her hair cut. Her mommy always used to cut it, but now Kit was nine and going to a new school and for a treat she was getting her hair cut by a real hairdresser. But it wasn't a treat. It was awful. The hairdresser had a low, gentle voice and asked if Kit wouldn't like a permanent. She'd look real nice with a few curls. She'd like it, she was sure. Kit knew she wouldn't like it. But she couldn't talk. She felt so dizzy, she thought she might fall outa the big chair. She used all her concentration just staying in the chair. She didn't have any left to say she didn't want a perm. Anyway, people seem to do what they want to you no matter what you say, if you're a kid. The lady said it was settled then, she'd give her a nice permanent wave.

Afterward, Kit started crying as soon as they got into the car. Somebody was inside her head pounding with a big hammer. And lights were flashing in front of her eyes. And outside her head, her hair was all wrinkled up in a stupid hairdo that she hated. And she couldn't do anything about it.

People just take you and do stuff to you, and you can't stop them, even though it's supposed to be *your* hair, not theirs. They shouldn't do that to little kids, especially when you can't talk 'cause you're so dizzy and sick.

7. All Straightened Out

Kit was very neat. Her skirts were in the left part of her closet and her shirts were in the right part. She had to wear skirts now that she was in a different school. Before, she went to the school her parents started so that kids who were different colors could go to the same school. All the other schools in Virginia then were for just one color or another. Kit's parents thought that was pretty weird, so they started another school. But now Kit couldn't go there anymore and she had to wear skirts. But she made her mommy make the skirts loose so they didn't stop her from breathing. Overalls were better for that, but she couldn't wear them anymore. She always thought being a boy would be better.

So anyway, I was telling you about her stuff. Her sea shells and sharks' teeth were all organized in a pear box and her rocks were in little boxes in an apple box. Each box had rocks from a different place. She wrote the names on the boxes. All her stuff was like that.

Except one thing she couldn't straighten out. Well, it wasn't really a thing. It was an idea. She needed to figure it out. She didn't like things that were messy or not finished. She thought about it. She knew it was a bad thing. So maybe it was easy to figure out. She just wouldn't ever do it. That was settled.

The next night, she thought about it again. Her first idea wouldn't work 'cause she would grow up and fall in love and get married. And married people did it even though it's bad. So she'd have to do it. Or maybe she and her husband could just not do it. They could get married but not do the bad thing. That was it! Why didn't everybody do that?

The next night she thought of another problem with her plan. That was how people got babies. So, when she was going to get a baby she'd have to do it. No matter how hard she thought, she couldn't get it all straightened out. Every night for a long time she tried to figure out what to do. Then one time she thought well, maybe it would be OK to do it just that once to get a baby. That's probably what people do. Finally she could go to sleep. She had it figured out. She never thought about it again for a long time.

8. Cancer

Kit heard on TV the Seven Signs of Cancer and finally knew what was wrong with her. She knew for a long time that she was bad and dirty and had a bad secret. That must be it. She had cancer. She couldn't tell anyone. She knew you can't tell your parents the really bad stuff. Everybody knows that.

9. Out for a Pass

Kit forgot what the big boy said to her, and while she was running she looked back to see if he was throwing the ball to her. They were playing football on the gravel playground between the church and the parsonage—that's the house where Kit lives.

When she woke up, she saw all the kids looking down at her. Someone was saying they should move that stupid volleyball pole out of the playground 'cause nobody played volleyball anyway; everybody played football. Somebody ran to Kit's house to get her mommy.

I would've taken Kit up through the ceiling when she got sick in her bed after that just like I always used to when she was little, but she didn't play with me anymore, even though I'm still magic. It wasn't just 'cause she was starting to get older than me—she was eleven. It was also 'cause she had a noise in her head that was in front of me and Little Kit and all the stuff we used to do. It was a noise like flashing lights, so Kit couldn't see back there. She didn't remember anything about us, even though we used to do lots of stuff together. So, I couldn't do anything to help her when she kept getting knocked out and getting sick afterwards or when she got stomach aches even when she didn't get knocked out. And her stomach aches sorta seemed like part of the noise and flashing lights in her head. It all seemed like one big thing to keep her away from me and Little Kit and all the stuff we used to do.

10. Bloody Rags

Kit wasn't sure which brother got stuck with the fountain

pen. She knew it was a mistake. Oh, they were mad at each other and they were flicking ink at each other on purpose. She just didn't know which one lost his hold on the pen and accidentally threw it at the other one. She just knew she had to get the blood off the floor before their parents got home from visiting shut-ins. Scott and Nash both disappeared. They were probably upstairs doing their homework.

Kit got a rag outa the rag bag on the basement door. She crawled around under the dining room table and cleaned up the spots of blood till she was sure they were all gone. Then she wadded up the bloody rag and wrapped it in a clean rag and then in a paper bag and then another paper bag. And then she ran across the playground to the church and stuffed the bag in the bottom of the trash can out back. She worked it down under some sticky paper tablecloths probably thrown out after the wedding yesterday. She didn't know why, but she knew just what to do.

11. Horse

Back when Kit was six, she got a new brother besides her two big brothers. He wasn't too much fun at first, but after a few years he got more fun to be with.

Kit and her little brother made up all kindsa games. One day they played cowboy and Kit was the horse. She had an idea that Kenny could go across the dining room and run and jump on his horse like a real cowboy. So, he did that. But he jumped too far and landed on Kit's head. Kenny couldn't wake her up and blood was coming outa her nose. He was scared and ran into the basement. Her nose never looked the same after that.

12. The Roof

"Now everyone get your pajamas on and get your pillow."

Kit's mommy looked like she had a special secret, like a Christmas present stored on a high shelf in the closet. Sometimes things got pretty fun when she had that look.

Everyone was Kit and her little brother Kenny. Scott stayed with another family now during the week so he could go to another high school. And Nash was at college.

When Kenny and Kit brought their pillows outa their bedrooms, there were Bill and Ruth standing on the stairway in their PJ's, too. They were stuffing blankets and foam pads out the window onto the roof. There was a part of the house that had two stories and a part that just had one story. And you could get to the flat roof of the low part from this window in the stairway.

"What are we doing?" Kit asked. She looked real worried.

"We're sleeping on the roof. It's a beautiful night," Ruth said.

They all climbed out the window and set up their little roof-beds. Kit did hers real quick and crawled under the blanket. She pulled it up over her face and didn't even look at all the stars. She heard everyone else talking about constellations—that's bunches of stars—but she didn't look. She was hiding. She wanted to say, "What will the neighbors think?" But she knew that was something parents are s'posed to say, not kids. So, she didn't say anything and just went to sleep as fast as possible. She could do that. When she was worried, sometimes she'd just lie down and put herself to sleep. That was the best way to get away. Kenny and Ruth and Bill had a lot of fun sleeping on the roof. I think Kit missed lots of fun things 'cause she worried.

13. Sledding

There was just enough snow that a sled could slide on it. Kit and Kenny were sledding down the little hill in back of the playground. There were bigger hills in the neighborhood, but they were scary. So, Kit and Kenny just used the little one next to their house.

It was Kit's turn—they were taking turns so they wouldn't bump into each other. Kit started a little bit farther to the left this time 'cause the snow was wearing out and getting muddy where they'd been sliding.

Part way down the hill, Kit got scared. She was heading straight for the concrete pipe that was sitting at the bottom of the hill. It was there for kids to crawl into and play in. She used to like going in there to hide. But she didn't like going toward it on a sled. She tried to push the handles and steer away but she couldn't. Maybe Kenny was yelling.

And then she was lying in the muddy snow sorta jumbled up against her sled and the big pipe. Kenny ran down and asked if she was OK. She couldn't think of anything to say. He ran to get their mommy.

While he was gone, Kit noticed that her sled runner was pointing right at her leg. In fact, she couldn't see all of it. It disappeared into her snowpants. She felt so dizzy and tired she thought she might just close her eyes and go to sleep. So she did.

Later, when Kit was lying in bed with a bandage on her leg, Kenny came in to see how she was. "Why didn't you jump off the sled?" he asked.

Kit didn't know.

14. Better than a Pillow

The doctor was holding a big nose-shaped thing over her face but he said he wouldn't put it on her. Kit didn't believe him. But he kept saying he wouldn't put it on her face. He'd just hold it nearby. Kit was real worried. But her mother was there to make sure everything was OK. Then the man put it right down over her face. It was real good for keeping her from talking 'cause it filled in all the spaces around her nose and mouth so no air could get into her. I'm pretty sure she died that time. Not right away. She kicked and thrashed and twisted. But she couldn't get away from that big man. She heard him saying stuff to her mother about a normal reaction and how she was doing it in her sleep.

Then Kit was up in a black sky, floating around a tall, golden pillar. Not exactly floating, though. She was gradually being pulled down toward a huge fire at the bottom of the pillar. She could see the flames 'way down there, and she struggled with all her might to keep from falling. There were a few other stars circling around the pillar with her. They all tried to stay up, but they were all gradually sinking down.

Kit got tireder and tireder. She felt heavier and heavier. She knew she was gonna fall into the fire 'cause she was getting lower and lower down the pole. But she didn't stop struggling until all her strength was used up.

Then she stopped fighting and fell into the red and orange flames.

But a strange thing happened. The fire was cool and Kit slipped through the flames like a feather floating in a breeze and landed softly on a green meadow that was underneath. Kit felt light and relaxed and safe. She lay on the soft, green grass and watched the other stars—they fell through the flames, too. They were dancing on their points in the meadow and jumping across stepping stones in a brook that made a gurgling noise. Kit felt silly for all the time she spent spinning around that pole trying not to fall into the fire. It was much worse up in the sky struggling to keep out of the fire. And this meadow was here all the time. She thought she would never leave that beautiful place. And then she shut her eyes and fell asleep on the grass 'cause she was so tired.

15. A Hole in the Wall

Kit was sitting in her room doing her homework. I was impressed by all the things she could do now that she was in high school. Like, she could figure out how long a piece of a triangle was. And she could forget things real fast, too. She was always real good at forgetting certain kindsa things, and she could still do that. Like, she already forgot that she threw the scissors at her father a few minutes ago. He jumped outa the way and they stuck in the wall. That's when she went up to her room. She was getting better and better at forgetting things. I don't know if her parents are as good or if they just don't talk about certain things. But nobody ever said anything about that hole in the wall.

Doing her homework, Kit could hear the record she put on the big wooden record player downstairs. Now it was at the song about Mr. Bojangles, a man who loved to dance. She was smiling 'cause she liked that song. It got to the part about how his clothes flapped all around, and then she put her head down on her geometry homework. Her eyes stung. She didn't know why.

16. Something Weird

The teacher asked Karl to read aloud. Kit thought that was pretty funny 'cause Karl was absent. But then his voice started reading the story. Kit turned and looked at the desk next to hers. Sure enough, there was Karl. Only, when she looked straight ahead he was gone. She experimented with other people. She could make them disappear by putting them at certain places in her eyes.

Suddenly she remembered about the story and looked in her book to find the spot. Only, her book didn't make any sense. It didn't have whole words in it. There was just a jumble of letters. She got worried that the teacher would ask her to read. What would she say: I'm sorry I can't read, my book doesn't have words in it? Kit felt her ears get hot. Finally the bell rang and it was time for lunch.

In the cafeteria Kit ate her sandwich and she told her friend who always ate lunch with her about the weird thing in English class and how glad she was that she didn't have to read. No, her eyes were OK now, she told Eileen. Then she put her hands on the table to push her chair away, but the table was gone. She looked down at her hands. They were right there on the table, but she couldn't feel it. That worried her. And now her head was starting to hurt and Eileen said she should go to the nurse. While she was walking to the infirmary she started feeling sick in her stomach.

By the time her mother came to take her to the doctor, Kit felt awful. Everything made her throw up and made her head hurt more. Her head felt as big as a basketball. Light made her sick. Moving her head made her sick. The noise of the nurse writing with a ballpoint pen made her sick. Looking at the chewed-up pieces of bologna and cheese in her throw-up made her sick.

The doctor touched her arms and legs with a sharp thing and a dull thing. He looked in her eyes. He told her to go home and rest. In a few hours she felt better.

17. Waterfall

Kit was feeling sick—the doctor said there was something wrong with her lungs—so she didn't go on the hike with the other college kids. They were going to walk to a glacier and swim in the lake beside it. Kit was cold just thinking about it. She stayed near the campsite and walked slowly along the path through the tall pointy trees. She looked over the edge, 'way down at the river that was made out of melted glacier. She couldn't see the edge of the river 'cause it was actually under the path right there. She looked at her feet. Was the path strong? What a stupid question. Of course it was. Lotsa people walk on this path. She just wasn't used to being in big mountains like this. She was used to the rounder mountains they have in the east.

Then some dirt broke under her foot and she fell down through the air until she landed in the river. She was very surprised, especially since she couldn't tell which way was up. She was a good swimmer and even a Red Cross Life Saver. But that doesn't matter if you can't tell where the air is and your arms and legs are flying around to places you didn't tell them to go. She felt like clothes in a washing machine.

Suddenly everything slowed down 'cause she crashed into a rock. She was holding onto it, and her legs swooped around and flapped behind her. She noticed that she was in a big river. She noticed that her arms were sliding on the rock. She realized she couldn't swim in this water that was jumping around like huge, wet monsters. She got real scared and tried to make her arms move the other direction on the rock. But they slid off instead and everything was fast again.

Then she was holding onto another rock and breathing real hard and her arms were slipping. She was gonna die. She knew that. But she held onto the rock as long as she could anyway.

Her arms slid off and then there was a strange thing. There was this extra hand and it was holding Kit's wrist. And she wasn't going away. Well, very slowly she was moving away from the rock. But then she started moving the other way. And pretty soon there was a whole man pulling her out of the water. They jumped from one rock to another and got to the edge of the river. Kit was shaking a lot. She turned around and looked at the river.

She was standing at the top of a waterfall. She looked over. 'Way at the bottom was a pile of huge rocks.

"I guess that water's pretty cold," the man said. Kit didn't know.

At the end of the summer, Kit went to visit her parents at their cottage at the church camp for ministers. She wanted to see them before she went back to college.

She slept in Aunt Minnie's room. That was the first time she didn't sleep in the children's room. Her parents said the double bed would be more comfortable. It was August and the nights were hot, but Kit ended up using all the blankets in the cottage and borrowing her mother's sweater to keep her warm at night. Everyone said she wasn't over being sick.

Kit didn't go back to college that fall. She didn't feel good and she stayed with her parents. When her aunt and uncle and cousins came to visit at Christmas, her parents made a suggestion. They said since her uncle was a pastoral counselor now—he didn't have a church anymore; he talked to people to help them with their problems instead—so, since he did that work now instead of preaching and stuff, maybe Kit would like to talk to him privately. Kit didn't really want to, but it seemed like it should be a good idea, like taking medicine.

Kit and her uncle walked across the gravel playground that still had the swings and the volleyball poles and the concrete pipe. They went into the church and sat in arm chairs in a little room. Ned asked Kit questions, mostly about sex. Kit didn't know anything about sex and she didn't like her uncle asking about it. She felt kinda sick and had a knot in her center, just under her heart. She thought maybe they'd talk about some stuff that was bothering her but instead Ned kept talking about sex. Once he said, "I see that your lips are dry. You're licking your lips a lot. Are you nervous?" Kit felt yucky. She didn't like anybody looking at her lips and making comments about them. She also wondered if her uncle was showing off what he learned in counselor school. But mostly she felt yucky. She felt the same way when Ned said she had her legs twisted around each other, crossing a buncha times, and wouldn't she be more comfortable if she untwisted them.

She was glad when the hour was up and they could go back to the house.

18. Iracles

"Do you want to see my gun?" Pantelis asked Kit. But she wasn't sure that's what he said 'cause her Greek wasn't that good. She knew she heard him right, though, when he put a black gun on the taverna table. (A taverna is like a little restaurant.) It looked cold and heavy. But she didn't touch it to see if it was. She didn't like it. She was beginning to think that she didn't like Pantelis either.

But he was Maria's cousin and the only person who could take her to Maria's father in the little village in the mountains. Kit promised to go visit Maria's father, Iracles, when she was studying in Greece. Maria loved her father but she didn't think she'd see him again 'cause he was old and she lived in America now and he was the only part of Greece she didn't hate.

Maria went to a lot of trouble to get to America. She walked a long way to go to a high school. Then she went to Athens and did whatever people told her so she could get a job and keep it. There weren't enough jobs for everybody, so you had to do what the men told you to do, even if you thought it was bad, if you wanted to get a job. Then a Greek family in America paid for her to come on a boat and live with them. She had to work for them for two years to pay them back and she never got to leave the house. It was bad and hard and not the way it was s'posed to be. Finally she paid them back and she got a job teaching Greek. That's how Kit met her, when she was getting ready to go study this thing called philosophy in Greece. (Don't ask me what that is.) Kit could tell from how hard Maria worked to get out of Greece that she really hated it there. But Kit didn't think too much about that till after she met Pantelis and saw the village where Maria grew up.

That's what she was trying to do there in the taverna in Athens, trying to get to Brallos, the village in the mountains. But instead, she was looking at a gun. Then Pantelis put it away. He said he worked for the KYP—that's like the CIA—but Kit thought he looked mostly like a little boy in a cowboy suit. Still, she was afraid of him.

Finally, Pantelis paid for his coffee and they left. But he didn't walk to a bus station or a train. He went into an apartment building. "Maybe he's getting his suitcase," thought Kit. They walked up some cement stairs and Pantelis unlocked a door. Inside was a nice apartment. Kit asked Pantelis if he lived there. He said no. Then he said it was time to eat. Kit said she wasn't hungry; she just ate. Pantelis said it was time to sleep then. Kit said she wasn't tired either, but he told her to go in the bedroom. So, she did. She lay down on the bed when he said to, but she didn't feel sleepy at all. She felt sick when he sat down on the bed next to her and put his hand on her hair. She couldn't understand everything he said, but she got the part about how he would be a brother to her. She squeaked out, "That isn't how brothers act in America," but he didn't understand 'cause she said it in English. She was having trouble figuring out what was Greek-ness and what was rudeness. She knew she didn't like Pantelis sitting on the bed but she didn't know if that was normal for Greece or if he was a bad man. She felt dizzy.

The telephone rang and he went into the other room to answer it. Suddenly Kit could think a lot better. She got up and put her sandals back on and went into the other room, too. She put on her backpack and said she was ready to go to Brallos. She felt much better when they got out onto the smelly street again. The diesel smoke felt fresh compared to the air in the apartment.

After a long time on trains and buses, Pantelis and Kit started walking across a rocky hillside full of stickery plants. Kit wished she had on real shoes instead of sandals, 'cause her feet were getting prickled. They were also getting cold 'cause it was nighttime.

Kit and Pantelis were the only ones who got off the bus there and they walked a long time away from the road. Kit started to wonder if they were really going to Brallos. She wondered if Pantelis still had that gun in his jacket. But just then she thought she saw a straight line in the darkness against the sky, like a roof. Then there were more lines. They were straight. They were little houses, a village.

When they got closer, Kit asked which house belonged to Iracles, Maria's father. Pantelis looked shocked and said didn't she know you can't go to your host's house after dark. She didn't know. But she could tell that must be a real bad thing to do. Pantelis said they'd stay at his mother's house. Kit waited outside while Pantelis went in. There was some talking, mostly Pantelis sounding like a bully, and then he came to the door and told Kit to come in. The hard dirt floor inside the house was just like the hard dirt outside. There was no light, but Kit had the feeling there wasn't much to see in the house. Pantelis told her to sleep in the other room. There were two rooms, the one you come into from the outside and the other one. She went into the other room.

Kit's eyes were pretty used to the dark from walking from the road, but it was even darker in the little house. She saw a sorta table. She touched it. There was a scratchy rug on it, actually two. She looked around. There was nothing else.

This must be the bed. She crawled between the rugs. After a few minutes she realized they were already warm when she got in. She wondered where Pantelis's mother was sleeping now. And where was Pantelis? Finally, even thinking about the black gun couldn't keep her awake.

In the morning, Kit walked into the main room but nobody was there. Her cotton skirt was all wrinkled. When she went outside she noticed three things: two bloody chicken feet lying on the ground and a big mountain with snow on it. The mountain where Brallos was ended with a cliff. After that there was a big space and then the big mountain with snow. It was pretty. Kit wanted to walk over to the cliff sometime and look over.

Then Pantelis and his mother were there and she was asking if he was sure Americans ate dinner first thing in the morning and he said she was just a stupid old woman who didn't know anything about the world. She didn't ask any more questions and brought Kit a bowl of rooster stew. So, those were rooster feet. Kit looked around and saw a couple of chickens in a cage but no rooster. Pantelis made his mother kill her rooster. Kit stood by the feet and tried to eat the stew, but she didn't feel hungry.

After breakfast-dinner, Kit asked where Iracles lived and Pantelis looked shocked again. You can't arrive at your host's house at this hour. Kit felt stupid. Pantelis took her to his aunt's house a little farther down the hill, to kill time while Kit waited till it was OK to see Iracles. They sat on wooden chairs and drank a syrupy drink. Then they went to another aunt's. They sat outside and ate stale little cookies with jam in them. Later, Kit thought they musta been pretty special cookies to be saved so long.

Every time they went to someone's house they ate or drank something even though they weren't hungry. And every time they left a house, Kit asked where Iracles lived and Pantelis rolled his eyes and explained how bad it would be to go see him right then. Most of the morning it was because Iracles was an important man in the village and was in charge of building the fire for the Easter lamb. Then he was killing the lamb and putting it on the skewer and raking the coals and all sorts of other things to do with the Easter feast.

Finally Kit saw that they'd been to every house in the village except the one closest to the cliff. So, she got her backpack and started to walk over there. Pantelis was shouting at her to come back, Iracles was too busy. She called back that she was sure Iracles would understand if she did something wrong. But she wasn't really sure.

When she walked up the hill toward the cliff edge—it went up before it went down—she saw a skinny man standing up there by himself. He didn't look too busy. He must be finished with the fire and stuff. When she got closer, she saw a bunch of chickens around him. He was smiling, which showed about four teeth and spaces for a lot more that weren't there. He was glad to see her.

Late that afternoon Kit and Iracles met the families from that end of the village and they sat on rocks around their fire by the cliff and looked at Mt. Parnassos and ate the Easter feast Kit heard so much about. The feast was just one thing, lamb. And because Kit was the special guest she got the first plate, which was just fat 'cause they weren't down to the meat yet. And there was just one thing to drink. It came in a little metal cup with a stem like a flower and it tasted like fire if you could make it liquid. I don't think anybody noticed Kit pouring her drink into the gravel by her rock. But a little girl saw a dog eating the fat Kit gave it. I think she told her mother, but I'm not sure.

The next morning, Kit found Iracles standing in front of his house when she got up. He had a big smile. He went inside and got two eggs died red—they make red eggs at Easter in

Greece. He told her she could stand out there and look at Mt. Parnassos and eat her egg and watch the chickens who gave it to her. He said he did that nearly everyday. He said his chickens gave him the sweetest eggs 'cause they were happy. They walked around on the hilltop and ate good food and breathed good air and looked at Mt. Parnassos on the other side of the valley. They didn't have to live cooped up in a cage like the other chickens in Brallos, and they thanked him by giving him sweet eggs.

Kit understood why Maria wanted her to meet Iracles. When he talked, it was like poems.

Back in Washington, D.C., Kit knocked on the dark green door. She knocked under the white number 402. The number was the only thing in the stairwell that wasn't dark. Maria opened the door and didn't say Hi! or Kit! or You're back! She said, "How could you do that to my father?" Kit thought about standing on the hill eating red eggs with Iracles and looking at happy chickens and Mt. Parnassos, and smiling at each other 'cause they couldn't talk so well with egg in their mouths and 'cause Iracles didn't have so many teeth and Kit wasn't so good at Greek anyway. She didn't know what Maria was talking about. "I never got *one* letter from Brallos after I left—my father can't write. Not one letter until you went there." Kit still didn't know what was going on. Maria picked up a pile of envelopes from a little table by the door. Kit was still standing on the landing. "Then I got a letter from *every* house in the village telling me what a fool my father had been made by the American girl and Pantelis."

When Maria figured out that Kit didn't know what this was all about, she wasn't so angry and she let Kit come in her apartment. She realized Kit musta been rude 'cause she didn't know any better. She just wasn't taught any manners when she was little. Maria explained all the bad things Kit did. She said when you go visiting you aren't supposed to talk to anyone else until you greet your host. You definitely shouldn't eat with anyone else till you eat with the person who invited you. And it was so bad to sleep in someone else's house first that she never heard of anyone doing that before.

Maria said that Pantelis was the big man in Brallos now, even though he really lived in Athens. And everyone was laughing at Iracles.

Kit felt awful.

But then she got mad at Pantelis. He tricked her. It was all his fault, scaring her with that gun and his gentle, low voice.

But then she thought it was her fault for missing the clues. Why could they visit *every* house in the village except Iracles's? Why weren't other people too busy to be bothered on Easter Day? And she shoulda noticed the lie about Iracles being an important man. Maria told her that Iracles didn't fit into the village and that people thought he was stupid 'cause he was gentle instead of fighting to be a big, important man. Kit wondered why she didn't notice those obvious things. All she could remember was how low Pantelis's voice was and how weak and confused she felt when he talked.

Then Kit thought about Iracles, a lonely old man standing on a hill with his chickens, listening to people laughing down by the other houses and telling the story again and again of how the American girl made such a fool of him.

She wondered if he still talked like poems. Maybe to his chickens.

19. Onions

Kit was eating a dish of vanilla ice cream 'cause that was the only flavor. All of a sudden she had a bad feeling. It was very strong, but she couldn't figure out what it was. It was something wrong with her mouth. It was heat or sharpness or flavor. She couldn't tell. But something was very wrong with her mouth.

Gradually she figured it out. Flavor. Hot spice. Onion. Very strong raw onion. That was it. She poked at her ice cream and found big chunks of onion. She told the waiter and he said, "No, that's impossible." She tried to show him but he just said it was impossible. Kit started to lose track of where she was. Things started to get thin and wobbly. And the universe got a crack in it.

She paid her bill and drifted out of the restaurant. The waiter ran up to her. He looked upset, like the universe might have a crack in it. He said there was onion in the ice cream, like he was the one who discovered it. Kit's universe came back together again and things got strong.

20. Trapdoor

Kit went down through the trapdoor and crouched at the top of the ladder so she could talk to her brother who was taking a shower in the basement 'cause that's where the shower was in his house. When they were done talking, she swung up so she could pop outa the trapdoor. Only, she hit the ceiling instead. When she woke up, there were drops of water falling on her face and she saw her brother's face with his hair hanging down in little points. And there was a square of light with more faces looking down at her. They all looked worried so Kit thought she'd say something reassuring like "I'm fine." But when she tried to say that, all that came out was a scary sound like a person moaning. So she didn't try to say anything else for a while. She got sick that time, too.

21. Break-In

The door was open. That was weird. Kit got kinda tense

when she walked in the room. Someone had been in there. All the kids at the school where Kit worked were in trouble, so this sort of thing happened all the time. But it was the first time anyone broke into Kit's room. She felt worse about this than she did about what they did to her car. She was lucky they were so messy about the car. They left the gas cap off and spilled white powder all over the ground, so she knew not to drive the car. She took the gas tank off—it was kinda hard 'cause the bolts and things were rusty—and she was gonna wash it out with gasoline. That was all she could think of to do.

But now someone broke into her room. It was her only private place, and now it wasn't private anymore. The apples were gone from the table. No big deal. She could pick some more. But the Swiss Army Knife was gone, too. Well, she could buy a new one but she probably wouldn't.

Then she looked at her desk. She could hardly breathe. She started to get dizzy. The cloth bag that she kept her journal in was missing. "Maybe they just moved it," she suddenly thought. She searched frantically around the room. It was gone. Kit started to feel sick. The place under the front bones got all tight. She wandered outside and looked up in the apple tree and then down the grassy hill to the pond and the woods. She went back in and searched the room again. There really weren't too many places to look. She went outside again. She had notebooks in that bag from five years. It felt like her life was in there. They stole her life. Why would they want it? She checked the room one more time and then went back outside. It felt like they stole her, the part that was all hers and not for anyone else.

She suddenly threw up under the apple tree.

22. The Smoker Who Doesn't Smoke

Eileen smoked two cigarettes while she talked with Kit. Kit

needed a new place to live. Eileen said the two of them could get a place together. Kit said she didn't want to live with cigarette smoke. Eileen looked surprised and said, "I don't smoke."

Kit looked at the dish she gave Eileen for an ashtray. It had ashes in it and two wrinkled filters with lipstick on them. She looked at Eileen. She looked back at the ashtray. She couldn't think of anything to say.

Everything started getting thin and wobbly.

23. Thick, Heavy, and Sharp

Kit lay in her bed. She had a thick, heavy feeling and she couldn't move. She could never tell if it was her or something else that was so heavy. And sharp, too. It was thick but sharp. She just thought that was a stupid feeling. Things aren't thick *and* sharp. And it was just dumb not to be able to breathe when you had that stupid feeling.

24. Pierced Ears

Kit drove her cousin to the drug store. While Mir was looking for what she needed, Kit went next door to the jeweler's. She thought she recognized the name of the store. She thought it was where her mother got her ears pierced. Kit was real surprised when she saw her 67-year-old mother with pierced ears. Kit always thought ear piercing was "barbaric mutilation" and probably dangerous. Also, jewelry was "frivolous and self-indulgent." Kit thought her mother thought these things, too. But then she got her ears pierced and seemed pretty happy about it. So, Kit just went next door to see if they pierced ears, you know, to see if this was the place her mother told her about. She was kinda bored and it was something to do.

"Do you pierce ears?" she asked.

"Sit down here," the man said, pointing to a stool. Kit sat down. He held a kind of gun up to her ear and shot a pointy earring through it. Kit didn't want earrings; she just wanted to know if this was where her mother came. But the man's voice was strong and kind, and she did what he said. Then he shot the other ear and the machine wouldn't let go. He struggled and pulled but couldn't get it off her ear. Another guy came over who worked in the store. He couldn't get it off either. Kit was trying to laugh so she wouldn't get scared. But she was already scared. The inside of her chest was getting tight and hard like a nut. Finally, three people were fiddling with the earring gun, and at last they got it off.

Kit walked back to the drug store. Miriam's mouth fell open like a cartoon

25. Soft Mommy

One day Kit and her mother were remembering about a time when Kit was little and the whole family went to Pennsylvania for Thanksgiving. They got to Grandpa's house and Raggedy Ann was gone. She musta fallen out the car window. While Kit and her mother were talking about that time, Kit's father was washing dishes and listening. Kit's mother said she'd never forget how upset Kit was. "You were crying and saying, 'What will my dolls do without their soft mommy?'"

That year, Kit spent Christmas with her parents. After eating oranges and special twisted up bread for breakfast, they opened their presents. Kit opened the box from her father and when she saw what was in it she suddenly felt real little and had to try real hard not to cry. It was Raggedy Ann, just like the one she lost out of the car window when she was little. It had red-and-white striped legs and red yarn for hair.

26. Trapdoor

Kit was at the boat house on the Potomac River in Washington, D.C. She was gonna practice with the team she was on. They were gonna row a long, skinny boat in a big race. They did that a lot. They had races with people from Canada and Mexico and Philadelphia and Australia and places like that. It's hard work rowing. Everyday, the team Kit was on practiced when it first got a little bit light till they had to go to work. Then they came back after work and rowed till it got dark again. Then they ran and lifted weights to make them strong and breathe a lot.

Kit had to get to the boat house before it got light so she could re-rig the boat. That means she had to use wrenches to move some parts so it would be right for her teammates. After practice she moved the parts back for the boys who owned the boat. Well, actually, it was their school that owned the boat.

This morning she was up on a high platform under the boat-house roof. She was getting some stuff she needed for the boat. When she was done, she put her hands on either side of the trapdoor and swung forward so she could drop down through the hole onto the workbench. But instead, she crashed her head into the end of a metal I-beam in the ceiling.

When she started to wake up, it was real slow. She could hear scratchy footsteps on the concrete floor. But that dirty floor sounded far away. Then she could see a bright patch. After a while, she realized that was the river showing through the big, square bay door. Finally, she realized where she was, lying on her side on top of the big platform up by the ceiling. Her feet were dangling over the trapdoor hole. Her teammates were wandering around down below, wondering where Kit was. But she couldn't talk for quite a while. Or move. And then she was too sick to row.

27. Abai

Kit fed all the animals in the classroom, the snapping turtle and the African clawed toad and the fish and the ring-necked doves and the spider and the chameleons... everything but the boa constrictor. It only ate once every three weeks. Then she washed all the glassware. Judy, who usually did this stuff with her had to go home early today. Now Kit was ready to go home.

But then Abai Belai came in and asked for help studying for the test tomorrow. He was ten. Kit was head of the science department at a school in Washington, D.C., for kids who were about ten to fourteen years old. School was over for the day, but Kit didn't mind staying to help Abai. She and Judy told their students they could always come after school and ask questions or help with the animals. Lots of them did.

Abai and Kit sat at one of the big wooden tables and looked at Abai's science notebook. It seemed like he knew everything real well. Pretty soon they were done. Abai was gonna do real well on the test. He closed his notebook but he didn't leave.

After a minute he asked, "Do you ever wonder about things?" Kit nodded. "Do you ever lie in bed and wonder about things?" Kit nodded and said she did. "Do you ever stay awake 'cause you can't figure something out?" Kit said she knew just what that felt like. "I've been wondering about something," Abai said. He looked at Kit to see if she was getting worried. He could always stop. But she didn't look worried. She looked interested, so he went on. "Why am I black and you're white?"

So that was it, Kit thought. It didn't have anything to do with the test. But she wasn't sure how Abai meant his question. She started off by saying that they had different genes, different instructions about how to look. He said he knew that but why did that make them different colors. He said someone told him he had melons in his skin. He seemed embarrassed to say that. He thought that person mighta been making fun of him 'cause of the stupid old joke about black people always eating watermelons. But he didn't even like watermelon. Kit said she didn't know if that person was making fun of him, but maybe he was talking about melanin, a chemical that gives color to skin and hair. Abai asked why he got more melanin than she did. She said that was where the genes came in. She drew a picture of how genes from parents can combine in different ways to make different kinds of children.

He said he understood how a chemical could give color like a dye and how genes for different amounts of dye could get passed on to children. But then he wanted to know how a gene, which just looked like a letter in the picture, could give him more dye. So she told him how the genes are recipes for different proteins like melanin in our bodies. He wanted to know who read the recipes, so she drew pictures to show how copies of the recipes are made and how molecules stick onto the recipes. It's chemical, not really like reading.

This took a long time to explain 'cause it's sorta complicated. But Abai understood it and he kept telling her to keep going when she asked if he wanted to know more. Kit was thinking that pretty soon Abai would know everything she taught the fourteen-year-olds.

"But I still don't know why I'm black and you're white. How did our parents get different genes and their parents all the way back?" So Kit told him about mistakes that are sometimes made in copying the recipes. And Abai wanted to know why her family had different mistakes from his family.

So, Kit told him the first people lived in Africa. In places where the sun is bright and people don't cover so much of their skin 'cause it's hot, it's important to be black. The color keeps the sun from giving you skin cancer. A baby who's born with a recipe mistake that makes him not so dark is less protected and may die of skin cancer before it can have a baby of its own. This kept the first people dark. The genes for light skin never survived. Abai said he understood, but then where did white people come from?

When some people moved north, Kit explained, they covered more of their skin to keep warm. That meant they didn't need so much color anymore to protect them from the sun and skin cancer. But they had another problem. The sun helps your skin make vitamin D, which you need to make strong bones. The people who went north had trouble making enough vitamin D 'cause so much of their skin was covered up. This made their bones weak and crooked.

So, if a baby in the north was born with a recipe mistake that makes its skin lighter, it was OK. It wasn't much in danger from skin cancer like white babies in the south. And it could make more vitamin D 'cause there wasn't so much color keeping the sun out of its skin. So, it made stronger bones than the dark children in the north. So, after a while all the people in the north were white, except people like Eskimos who got lots of vitamin D from the livers of the animals they ate.

Abai thought that was pretty interesting that being white in the south was dangerous and being black in the north was dangerous. He wondered if he was in danger since he wasn't in the south, not Africa anyway. Kit said he was OK if he drank milk with vitamin D in it. He said he liked milk and he'd check the carton to see if it had vitamin D in it.

And that was about it. Abai got the answers to his

questions in layers, all the way down till he knew enough for right then. Kit was surprised how much he wanted to know and how fast he learned really hard things. Even so, it was after 7 o'clock when they finished. They'd been talking for four hours. "Genetics. Molecular biology. Evolution," Kit was thinking. "We covered the territory of modern biology."

Kit was thinking something she thought a lot, that maybe schools were set up wrong, even the good ones like the one she worked in. Kids learn real complicated stuff when it's the answer to something that keeps them awake at night. Otherwise, it's hard and boring for them to learn it. Maybe kids should just be allowed to ask questions instead of all learning the same thing at the same time. It was hard to know how to set things up for kids. They had to be somewhere when the grown-ups were away, but sometimes they just looked like prisoners in school.

28. The Man, the Cop, and the Back

Kit was driving to the boat club on the Potomac River to practice with her team. Of course, first thing she'd do is re-rig the boat. I liked to watch Kit do all this stuff, but, of course, she didn't know I was still there.

Sometimes I still tried to talk to her. But that would turn on the migraine machine. Then she couldn't hear anybody.

There was this one guy who lived with Kit. He could turn on the migraine machine lots of ways. He said the opposite of the things she said and told her she had dumb ideas so she better use his ideas, and when she felt sad or scared he said she didn't feel that way, like he knew better than she did how she felt. Once when she thought she should leave him, he said she couldn't 'cause he was gonna make her "someone." He also said he loved her. All those different ways worked.

So, this time when she was driving to the boat house, it was dark 'cause she had to re-rig the boat before her teammates got there. She was crying 'cause that man didn't come home the night before. And then she saw flashing lights behind her. That scared her and she jumped in her seat. The police kept her at the side of the street for hours. She missed practice. I guess they thought something was suspicious 'cause she was crying so much.

A few weeks later—oh, the mean man never came back—the women's crew was ready for its workout but there was a bunch of junk in the way of their boat. They tried to lift the boat out of its rack and weave it up and over all the stuff, but they got stuck while Kit happened to be bent over a sawhorse, holding her piece of the boat at her ankles.

Two weeks later she still couldn't walk. But that was later.

The first *day* after the accident, Kit woke up and tried to get out of bed. At first she couldn't roll over. But finally she got on her side and figured out a way to slide her feet to the floor while the rest of her was still on the bed. It was hard to get dressed for work but she did it. Then she figured out how to get to the living room by sliding around on the walls since her legs couldn't hold her up by themselves.

She was very excited that morning because she was going to take her eighth-grade environmental science students on a canoe trip. They'd been building up to this for months. They listened to bird calls and looked at leaves. They studied live fish and dead ones.

Kit's mind was full of lists. She slid around the living room to the front door and along the outside wall of the house to her car. She eased herself behind the wheel and started to drive to school. She was thinking about the lunches she had to pick up from the kitchen and the canoe trailer she had to hitch to the van and the bus driver who needed a map. There were the life jackets and clipboards and borrowed binoculars and the seine and buckets...

And then she realized she could probably step on a pedal about five more times before her leg would stop working. She could tell it was really her back that had the problem but it would be her leg that stopped working. She made the car go slow and rolled past stop signs and red lights. She was looking for a pay phone. Finally she saw one on the side of a building. She drove right up over the curb and stopped next to the phone.

It was harder to get out of the car than it was to get in. She walked her hands down the hood, leaning as much weight on them as she could. Then she lunged at the phone and caught her balance. She called the mean man and he said he was busy but maybe he could come and drive her home in a couple hours.

Then she called the school but she fell down just when someone answered. By the time she got up, the person hung up. She dialed again and started crying. The person who answered sounded worried when all she heard was crying. But then Kit started talking about lunches and clipboards and the canoe trailer. The other woman kept asking if she was OK. Finally that woman said, "I'll take care of all the arrangements," to get Kit to stop talking about all that stuff, I guess. "Where are you? I'll come get you." But Kit wouldn't say 'cause she was embarrassed and the man who loved her was going to save her, even though he lived with someone else now.

Finally Larry came. Kit couldn't get out of her car. Her legs wouldn't work. He pulled her out and she used her hands to walk herself around her car and throw herself at his. He didn't try to help even though she fell down by his car and had to pull herself in the doorway by grabbing the seat and the glove compartment. Kit figured he didn't want to embarrass her. When they got to her house, he didn't hang around. Kit figured that was for the same reason.

After a while, Kit remembered that the phone was by her bed, so she called the doctor who was an oarsman at the same boat house where she rowed. The lady said the next appointment was in two weeks, and Kit said OK. She didn't think of telling her it was an emergency. And she didn't think of calling any of her friends or her parents who lived in the next town.

She always did that. She thought people knew about her problems and if they didn't help it was 'cause they didn't want to, like that time she was a student teacher in Massachusetts. She was supposed to have breakfast ready for the headmaster's children at 7 o'clock, and the teacher she worked with told her to be at school at 7 o'clock. So, she tried to make the kids eat a little early and then she ran the two miles to school, but she was always late. The teacher and the headmaster and his kids all seemed disappointed in her. Except Nat, the headmaster's youngest son. He liked her anyway and showed her his special things like his mice and his skull collection. Kit never said anything to anybody about her problem 'cause she figured they knew. Years later, she found out they didn't know. The teacher didn't know that Kit did house work and child care for the headmaster in exchange for room and board, and the headmaster didn't know that the teacher told Kit to be at school two hours early to set up stuff in the classroom.

So, anyway, she was lying in her bed with a hurt back, and she didn't tell anyone. When she had to go to the bathroom, she rolled off the bed and landed on the floor and cried which made her back cramp more which made her cry more. Then she pulled herself across the hall to the bathroom and she climbed onto the toilet. It was hard or maybe impossible to get back in bed, so she pulled some covers down and finally fell asleep on the floor.

She had a lot of time but she didn't remember anything.

She never even noticed that she was really hurt. And no one else did either 'cause she only told Larry and he didn't notice and school was out for two weeks for spring vacation.

29. No Expectations

The class was going great. Kit's eighth graders were asking questions about relativity and Kit was drawing pictures of trains and lights on the board and the kids were jumping up and adding things and every once in a while one kid's eyes would open real wide and he'd just stop talking for a minute. That was the part Kit liked best, when the eyes did that.

So, then these two guys dressed like lumberjacks walked into the classroom and everyone looked at them. One of them handed Kit a rose. It looked kinda funny in his big, rough hand. He said, "This is from your friend in Alaska." Kit couldn't think of anyone she knew in Alaska. The lumberjacks walked away. The kids were all grinning and whispering. Kit was real confused. She ran into the hallway and caught up to the men. "Who sent the flower?" she asked them. Only one of them seemed to know how to talk, and he only knew how to say one thing: "Your friend in Alaska." Kit tried to think of anyone she knew who might have *moved* to Alaska.

"Baker. Is his name Baker?" That guy who used to be what's-her-name's boyfriend. Didn't he move to Seattle? Maybe... Oh, this is ridiculous.

The talking lumberjack finally broke his program and said, "Baxter. Steve Baxter." Good Grief, it *was* that guy, the one who went to Washington State. Kit wanted to get his address and write him a thank-you note, but the lumberjacks just kept walking this time, and she had to get back to her class.

Well, a few days later, Kit got a card from Steve. So she wrote and thanked him for the flower. Then he called her and suggested she come visit. He'd pay 'cause he had lots of money. He called money "fun tickets." It was kinda exciting to think of going to Alaska, but it didn't seem like a good idea to Kit since she didn't really know Steve, so she said no thanks. But he called her some more and finally Kit said, well, she was going to be in Seattle for a little while in July and how about they meet there and go backpacking for a couple days. Later, Kit thought she better make sure that Steve knew that she really just wanted to go on a hike with him, not be boyfriend and girlfriend or anything. She was amazed she really did this, but she called him up to say that. And Steve said, "Of course. No expectations. We'll just go for a hike. Sounds great. No expectations." Kit felt relieved that he understood and proud that she made it clear.

So, there they were in a tent up in the Cascade Mountains and Steve was talking about Alaska and how violent it is there and how common rape and murder are, especially rape. And people there think differently about violence; it's just part of life. And about the law. They just sorta don't believe in laws. And sex. It's just good, violent fun.

Kit was scared. She couldn't think of anything to do. There was no one else around. And she had no feeling in her arms. They got real heavy and she couldn't move them. That sick, hard lump came in the middle of her chest.

Then Steve started talking about Vietnam and his job there during the war. His sentences got all mixed up and didn't make a lot of sense, but Kit got the part about how he went around to houses and beat people up and sometimes killed them if they didn't answer his questions. He had a person with him to put the questions in Vietnamese. Sometimes the people answered the questions but he just killed them anyway.

Then he said they oughta do the bad thing and Kit was real

surprised when she heard her voice saying real calm, "No, I don't feel close enough to you." Her heart was pounding like a boxer but her voice came out so casual. She talked real relaxed-like for a while and then turned over and pretended to be asleep. But she didn't go to sleep. She just lay there until she thought it might be a little bit light and then she got up and packed her pack. When Steve got up and found her packing, she said she was gonna walk out to the road and he could do what he wanted. So they walked out and drove back to Seattle and didn't talk. Kit was tense.

When they pulled up in front of the house where Kit was staying, Steve started talking and Kit didn't move. He got real mad and was yelling at Kit that she was a bad person and that he left his house and told his friends in Alaska that he didn't know if he was coming back 'cause he was going to meet a woman in Seattle and he might go home with her to Virginia. He called her names and yelled a lot. Kit couldn't talk, but she was wondering about no expectations. Pretty soon she couldn't quite see Steve's face or hear his words. And everything got thin and wobbly.

30. Shocked

Kit and her friends who were biologists saw lots of pretty birds in Palenque. That's an old place in the jungle in Mexico. Kit liked the birds. She also liked one of the biologists. She thought she might fall in love with him. But she was also getting sick. She started throwing up and going to the toilet a lot.

One day everyone else got hungry and she got sick. They took her to the little room where they were all staying and then they went away to get some food. Kit thought she might feel better if she got cleaned up. She went to the bathroom.

Sometimes, bathrooms made Kit sick and dizzy. She really

didn't like taking baths or showers because of this. But even though she was already sick, Kit didn't feel worse in this bathroom. It wasn't like the ones she was used to. It didn't have a sickening, hard, white tub and a tile floor and a shower head with a long metal arm and all that other white stuff that makes you feel sick. This bathroom just had a pipe in the ceiling over the toilet. You could turn the handle up there and water would pour down all over the toilet and the floor.

She washed herself and water collected on the floor 'cause the drain didn't work too well. The water looked pretty dirty, and scum and hair and toilet paper and cockroaches floated in it. That made Kit's stomach feel bad after all, even though nothing was white.

When Kit was done, she turned the handle in the ceiling to stop the water coming out and she dried off except her feet which were standing in the yucky water. Then she reached up to pull the light chain.

When she opened her eyes, she was lying in the dirty water and looking at brown stuff stuck under the toilet bowl about two inches away. Her left arm ached like it just did a million pull-ups. She threw up before she could get her head up over the toilet.

She felt like she'd been dead. She was glad her friends didn't come back and find her dead, naked body in the filthy bathroom. Since she was alive again, she could get clean and put her clothes on, and they would never know.

31. Trapdoor

The Wheat Thins must be on this aisle with the other crackers, but Kit wasn't finding them. She backed up a little and a little more, letting her eyes run up and down the shelves of boxes.

And suddenly her tailbone was bumping down some steep

steps real fast. And then she was sitting on the cellar floor. She was mighty surprised. She took a minute to check things out. It was dark down there. But there was a square of light at the top of the steps. The trapdoor was open. Then there were faces in the bright square.

Her tailbone hurt, and her legs felt wobbly when she stood up, and the bright light overhead made her feel a little sick. But she was pretty OK. Mostly just embarrassed and wishing people would go back to shopping. The store manager looked more scared than she did. I guess he thought he was gonna get sued.

The strangest thing, weirder than stepping through the trapdoor, was that Kit didn't even recognize that she'd done this before. She didn't even recognize the bright square.

32. The Man, the Cop, and the Back—Again

It was snowing real hard which was weird 'cause the lilacs were blooming and the hummingbirds were back. And it was dark which was not weird 'cause it was night. Also, the street was steep and slippery. So Kit decided not to try to stop when the light turned yellow. After she turned, she saw flashing blue lights in her rear-view mirror. She felt sick and started to cry more. She was already crying 'cause she was driving away from the little cabin where she and Vance had lived for two and a half months. He didn't want her to live there anymore. She could tell. He didn't talk to her even if she asked him a question. So, she didn't ask him questions anymore. When he came into the main room, he looked upset and crowded. Kit went into the bedroom and sat on the bed—'cause that was the only place to sit—to get out of his way. Then when he came into the bedroom and squeezed by the bed to get to the toilet, Kit went into the main room. She felt like she was always in his way. She wasn't doing it right. She was making him uncomfortable.

Kit moved to Colorado to spend the rest of her life with Vance. So she didn't want to be hasty. Maybe the rest of her life was over 'cause she was leaving. She was going to spend the night with a woman in Vance's address book. She didn't have any friends here. She didn't know Nancy. But when Kit called, Nancy said come stay with her.

The policemen asked her a lot of questions and kept her at the side of the road for hours. She tried to stop crying every time they went to their car and did cop stuff. She tried to think of the worst thing they could do so she would be ready. She decided it was to make her pay a bunch of money. She was wrong. The little one who was a woman came back and said Kit would have to go to jail. Kit couldn't even talk, she was crying so much. The cop walked away. It was snowing all the time and covering up Kit's car. Much later, they came back and said they got permission not to take her to jail. They gave her a ticket and talked to her a lot about how serious it was. Then they went back to their car.

Kit kept trying to get ready to drive and then she'd start crying again. Finally, the big cop who was a man knocked on her window. He said they couldn't leave until she did. Kit said she didn't think she could drive. Then the cop did an interesting thing. He punched her in the shoulder so hard that she fell over, and he said, "Pull yourself together!" I guess it worked 'cause she wiped the breath off the windshield and turned on the wiper and drove away. But she couldn't read the road signs, partly 'cause her eyes weren't working too well and partly 'cause the signs were covered with snow. So, she had to stop a lot and brush them clean so she could figure out where to go.

The next day, Kit went to the garage where her stuff was stored since she moved from Virginia. Her shoulder hurt from the policeman hitting her. She got a couple things she needed while she was staying on Nancy's floor. Then she started to open the garage door to get out. Just over her head, it broke and came crashing down. It hit her sore shoulder on the way down. When the pain got less she stood up and bent to try the door again. Since the spring on one side was broken, the door felt much heavier. It hurt her back to lift something that heavy, ever since that time at the boat house. Just over her head, it broke again—the other side this time—and fell on her head and shoulder. It was longer till she got up this time.

Now she was really trapped inside. She climbed up on her stuff to the top of the garage and looked out the little window. Could she break it and jump out? What a stupid idea! She climbed back down and tried the door. Too heavy. I think you call the next part panic. She went back up to the window and jumped down and tried the door. She went up and down a bunch of times, faster and faster. And then she grabbed the door handle and yanked it up a few inches. She wiggled her legs under, then held the door with her back and rolled hard under it as it fell shut. She was lying in cold, muddy slush and was free.

The next day she couldn't walk.

But this time she didn't have a job to get to or a house to hide in or lists to remember or anything. She noticed that her back was really hurt. She even noticed that she'd done this part before. And she noticed that she felt like an orphan. But that didn't make any sense. Her parents always loved her. But she still felt like a little girl locked out of the cozy house where everyone was singing by the fire. That was the beginning.

Part III

GETTING READY TO REMEMBER: BEAR TRACKS

(1984-1987, Kit)

Long before Columbus probed the world's edge, the Chinese, seeking an ideograph to represent the turning point we call "crisis" in English, performed a miracle of linguistic compression by combining two existing characters, the symbol for "danger" and the symbol for "opportunity", to create the character "we-ji", which stands as an eternal assertion that, since opportunity and danger are inseperable, it is impossible to make a significant move without encountering danger and, obversely, the scent of danger may alert us to the fact that we may be headed in the right direction.

James Lipton, "Here be Dragons", *Newsweek,* Dec 6, 1976

1. The Beast

The woman in Vance's address book, Nancy, could see I was pretty upset when I arrived at her house in the snowstorm. She asked if I would like to talk with someone. That's how I met Georgia. She's Potowatamee and a therapist.

Funny, although I was desperate to get help, I was certain that my situation was hopeless. The first time I met Georgia, I described how things were for me. I was 35. I fell in love. I saw a chasm before me. I was on the safe side. On the other side lay the mysterious, wonderful land of a committed relationship. I had never thought of trying to make the leap before, but this time I knew I would. And I wasn't going to make some half-hearted attempt so I could claim I could have made it had I really tried. No, I put everything I had into that jump. I sailed across the chasm. My toe touched the opposite cliff. I had made it! But just then, the cliff receded from my foot, leaving me to fall into the pit. I had been swindled. I did everything right and made it, but then the cliff moved. It wasn't fair. It was a cheat. And I was at the bottom of an impossibly deep hole with sheer sides and no way out.

I stopped. Georgia waited to be sure I was finished. She looked excited.

"That's great," she said incongruously. "If cliffs are moving, why, anything can happen. You could make the cliffs even higher... or lower. You could make a tunnel or a ramp. The pit could become a mountain. What a wonderful, mobile landscape you're in."

I was stunned. She had not imposed on me unwanted advice or pretended cheeriness. She had found the flexibility in my own rigid image, the mobility in my psychic landscape, and simply pointed it out to me. She showed me the solution embedded in my own formulation of the problem, the exit I had built into my own prison. Now, I didn't immediately feel great. I can't say I even felt hopeful. But I felt the hint of a glimmer of the possibility of future hopefulness.

Vance had moved to Washington State and I had moved back into the little cabin.. I couldn't explain why, but I wanted to do it. Not having a reason was reason enough not to do it, but Georgia smiled and asked how I felt about the possibility of living there. I felt great about it. I really wanted to live there, on the hillside next to the thickety draw. I'd looked at another place, modern, bigger, windows that actually keep the wind out, bathtub, no holes in the floor. Georgia asked me what chance a bathtub has against magic. I hadn't thought of magic, didn't actually believe in it. But it was a nice poetic word for a place that feels good. So, against the advice of my sensibleness, I moved back to the cabin.

One day, Georgia asked if I ever eavesdropped on what I said to myself in my head. I told her I didn't think I said *anything* to myself in my head. But the seed was planted, and one day as I dropped a spoon I had just washed, I overheard a scathingly sarcastic voice say, "That was smart. You'll have to wash it again now." Truly shocked, I began to listen more often to the commentary of this internal voice. It was ruthless. If someone else had spoken to me in that way, I'd have thrown him out of the cabin. But this was me.

Over the next week or two, no longer, I did nothing about the voice but listen. I didn't try to prevent it from speaking but just listened to its devastating judgmentalism. It was an utter perfectionist, allowing no room for errors, second thoughts, changes of mind, development, or experiment. No down time. No risks. And, therefore, no room for learning. I could hardly believe what I was discovering in myself. I don't approve of this sort of treatment of a human being. And here I was doing it to myself. The implications were obvious about blocking new experience, preventing novel approaches to familiar problems, stifling creativity, stiffening defenses against helpful criticism, undermining my self-confidence, and generally souring me to life.

But, at Georgia's suggestion, I let the voice speak. I didn't forbid its comments and therefore drive it farther underground. And, as a result, a miracle happened. Within a few days, the voice was all but silent, even in the situations which in the past had made it most virulent, like when I broke a pencil point or stumbled over my words as I spoke with a sales clerk or spilled flour on the floor. Simply bringing it into the open had been enough to shock it into stopping.

Just to check, I tuned in that channel from time to time in the following months, but the broadcast was over, the station had gone off the air.

At another meeting, I asked Georgia how she knew where to begin with a new client. She shrugged and said it didn't really matter. All the threads lead to the same core. So, you just pick up the one that's handy. The one that's lying there is the one that's ready.

Georgia suggested I close my eyes and let my awareness drift through my body, noticing any sensations but not lingering anywhere. Then she asked me to allow my awareness to be pulled to whatever place seemed to draw it. I was having trouble following her instructions because I kept thinking about the ache in my left shoulder. I tried to block that distracting sensation so I could do the experiment

Georgia was suggesting, to let my awareness be drawn... Oh, that *was* what was drawing my awareness. But it's so... unimportant. It's just my shoulder. Shouldn't it be something significant and central like my heart or my forehead?

I relaxed and let my mind settle in my shoulder.

A fire smoldered deep in the tissues. It flared and shifted, skittering to a slightly different spot as I focussed on it, elusive like a frightened animal.

Georgia asked if she could put her hands on my shoulder. And suddenly I was in the house where I grew up, the parsonage next to the gravel playground. A two-year-old in corduroy overalls stood mutely at the foot of the stairs. She looked at me, then to left and right. Her eyes turned again toward me. Something pushed from behind those eyes, something that wanted to be known. The little girl began to walk about the house. I followed. She wanted to show me something or tell me something.

Suddenly, outside the kitchen she turned into a filthy, ragged orphan. She squatted in the dark corner, afraid to look toward the warm glow coming from the kitchen doorway. Her mother was in there. The stinking orphan knew that she was too dirty to go into the glowing kitchen or to touch her mother.

Wait a minute, protested the intellectual part of myself. How can an orphan have a mother? And who is this little girl anyway? The question hung in the air as the orphan turned back into the blond two-year-old with the serious face. She looked at me incredulously through that question, her stare burning into me. Gradually the obvious answer came to me. This was myself. This was me, as a two-year-old. And she, I, had something to tell me, but she couldn't get it out or I couldn't take it in, what with all these distractions like her suddenly becoming a squalid orphan.

Then, confirming my thoughts about distractions, she

turned into a goat, strode into the radiant kitchen and peed on the clean, linoleum floor. I could hardly bring myself to tell Georgia what was happening; it was so simultaneously disgusting and funny.

But when was the little girl going to get to the message that she so obviously wanted to deliver?

Eventually, returned to her original form, she went to the stairway and, after some thought, began to climb to the second floor. A chill shimmered my muscles as the Little Girl ascended the dreadful stairs. Dreadful? How peculiar. This was my own childhood home, the site of many happy memories. And yet it was with a leaden sense of foreboding that I watched the earnest little blond move bravely up the steps. She disappeared into darkness at the top. My breath stopped. Where had she gone? The air hung still and heavy, but I couldn't take any of it into my lungs.

Then, swooping down the staircase directly toward me flew a screaming, black, leather-winged beast. It was, I knew, the Little Girl, me, horribly transformed. It belched flames and veered into the living room, flying wild circles through the claustrophobic space, slicing furniture and curtains with its sharp wing edge, scorching window frames and blistering paint with its flaming breath. It flew feverishly into every room in the house before turning straight up and bursting through the roof in a fiery explosion. The beast, finally free, flew an ecstatic spiral above the house and the church next door. My last view of the beast was as she loomed large and fierce against the church steeple.

I felt tingly after that session, the way your foot feels after it's been asleep, but also disappointed (although Georgia didn't seem to be) since all the commotion had prevented the Little Girl from telling me her message.

Several weeks after that, I got a severe headache. It wasn't a migraine, but it was a bad headache. It seemed as if a network of tiny channels in my brain was throbbing dangerously toward bursting. I paced. I pressed my forehead against the wooden wall. I grabbed my face and tried to push out the pain. I sat down and clamped my head between my hands, digging at my scalp with my fingernails.

Just then, I felt another digging, claws into the meat of my shoulders. My hands fell from my head. Fear tightened a band around my chest. The horny tip of a long beak touched the top of my head. Hot breath came from it. This was not normal. I resisted and the fear band tightened. The beak continued to rest lightly on my head.

Well, maybe this was OK. Georgia was encouraging me to allow my imagination more room. Maybe the beast—yes, it was the black, leathery beast, I suddenly realized—could do something to help. Maybe it had some power... Well, that was certain; it had power. But maybe it had some gentle power that could cure my headache. What a foolish idea. It isn't even real. The claws dug deeper into my shoulders. The beak tip still rested on my scalp. Yes, maybe it could rub my head gently and make me feel better. I see. Yes, I see.

Then, as if to convince me that I didn't see, the Beast leaned heavily on its beak so that it pressed uncomfortably against my head. I resisted, squinted, gritted my teeth against the pain. Hey, I thought... well, since you're part of me, I thought you'd be on my side, an ally or something. Why are you torturing me? The weight increased and with it the pain until my resistance collapsed. The strap around my chest snapped, I inhaled deeply, and the Beast's beak slid into my skull. The pain, surprisingly, lessened. OK. I see. The pain was in the resistance. I get it. I see. Sort of surgery, to let the headache out. I'll be fine now. Hey, this is great. Great.

The Beast withdrew its beak. I was enormously relieved at its departure, despite my nervous declaration of its helpfulness.

Oh no. It pressed again on another spot on the top of my head. The pain was excruciating. But again, as I weakened past resisting, the beak glided easily into my brain. Great. Symmetry. I see.

But the beak started on a third spot. Then a fourth. Gradually, either I became too tired to fight or I began to trust that this operation was good even though my attempts at understanding it had failed. Eventually, I lay limply against the tall back of the chair and waited with interest as the Beast drilled ten or a dozen shallow holes through my skull. I no longer resisted, no longer explained, and the drilling no longer hurt.

Then the Beast turned to the right and plucked a flower from the air. She placed it in one of my head holes and tweezed the bone and skin around the base of the long stem to hold it erect.

Immediately, as she plucked another flower, I felt roots begin to grow from the first. Tiny, thread-like roots pushing microscopically into my brain. As the flowers collected on my head, the micro-massage of the roots began to have its effect. The headache faded and eventually disappeared. I sat for perhaps an hour in the comfortable chair, smiling at the tall flowers sprouting from my head.

I thought maybe I would never have a headache again since I now had my flower roots massaging my brain. Anyway, I could always call the Beast back for more help.

Sometimes in subsequent weeks I did feel those roots sort of tickle away a potential headache. But that didn't always happen. And even though I invited the Beast back, she didn't come when I called. Not in her nature, I guess.

A letter arrived from Vance. It was full of blame, a category which was seeming less and less useful to me. Seemed to me that we humans hurt each other out of our own fear and pain. A person might be sad or angry about it, but it didn't seem like anyone's fault. I sat on the couch—which was a piece of plywood set on two melon crates and topped with three cushions from a dumpster—and read his letter. My stomach tightened. My hands tensed.

Then I felt claws grasp my shoulders. They were obviously supporting a heavy weight. But I didn't feel burdened. I felt energized. The claws dug deliberately into my flesh as the Beast unfurled its wings on either side of my head. My mouth opened slightly. Hot breath passed my lips. I became aware of the Beast's black, leathery body and of its pterodactyl-like head and long, toothed beak. Its mouth was slightly open and exhaled heat. Fire shot out in front of my face. My black beak remained loosely open and red-orange flames slid by my pointed teeth and billowed into the air. My black arms with their expanses of lofting leather stretched out energetically just above shoulder height. I looked at the letter in my lap and wondered why it wasn't an ash. My hands moved to crush it. Good manners arrested the motion for a moment before I crumpled the paper and threw it across the tiny room. A flame shot after it, singeing the air, purifying it. I stood up, for the first time in my own home. The air smelled clean.

I lived there seven years.

2. The Confession

My cousin Carol invited me to come to dinner one night while her father and his new wife were visiting her. We barbequed hamburgers in the backyard of her little brick row house in Denver and sat and talked into the long, summer evening.

Just as I was shifting in my chair, getting ready to leave, my uncle said as if he'd been building up to it all evening, "I have a confession to make." I stopped mid-motion and looked warily at him. "I've been carrying this guilt with me for years, Kit, about hurting you." A hard nut formed at my solar plexus.

Unaccountably embarrassed, I strained to think what he might be referring to and wished he'd hurry and get this awkward scene over with. It was always so difficult to get away from him; he always had just one more convoluted thought to deliver in his maddeningly ponderous tone. And the later the hour, the more embarrassing that thought was apt to be. Unbidden, the notion strayed into my mind like an untethered pony: "I'm glad I grew up listening to my father's sermons and not Uncle Ned's. Poor Carol."

"I don't know if you remember a time," my uncle continued, "when your family and ours went camping at Piseco Lake in New York State."

Our two families had always spent the summer months together, sometimes traveling but usually staying at the church camp in Pennsylvania where my paternal grandfather, also a minister, had built a small cottage. I wasn't sure which summer Uncle Ned was referring to. Still anxious about the mysterious confession, I settled into my lawn chair for the long, dramatic rendering of "The Camping Trip at Lake Piseco." Uncle Ned never chatted. He delivered theatrical monologues.

"We were all there, in the beautiful Adirondack Mountains, your parents and brothers, or perhaps just Kenny. The older boys might have been away. But you and Kenny and your parents and all of us T's were sitting by the fire after supper. It was a fine blaze on a chilly mountain night. You'd have been about nine or ten years old. You were sitting on the ground, so I offered you a folding camp stool. Oh, Kit, how I have regretted that since."

So that was it. I remembered the night well. Uncle Ned had thoughtfully lent me a stool. After sitting on it awhile, I decided to move closer to the fire. Gripping both sides, I scooted forward, holding the stool against my bottom and not bothering to stand fully upright. When I planted myself in the warmer spot, the stool, having unhitched its fastenings, collapsed under me, clamping the fingers of my right hand in a crossing of wooden bars. The pain was nauseating, blinding.

"You were in terrible pain." My uncle was finishing his tale. "I felt horrible. Ever since, I've carried the guilt of that evening with me. All these years..."

"You know what I remember about that night?" I interrupted. "You were the one who finally got that stool off my hand. No one else could do it. My father was struggling to pry it off, but you were the one who did it.

"So, please set that one aside, Uncle Ned." I hurried on, relieved that the anxious waiting was over and that the story hadn't been embarrassing after all, only a bit perplexing. Why on earth would he feel so guilty about lending me a stool? His feeling of remorse seemed genuine but somehow misplaced. "Don't spend any more guilt on that one," I pleaded. "In my memory, you were the hero of the evening. I've never had any anger at you about that silly incident." True, I hadn't been angry about it, but for some reason my words sounded like a lie. Perhaps because they were delivered more as an escape than as reassurance to my uncle.

In a phone conversation the next day, Carol told me her father had made a similarly puzzling confession to her. He explained that when she was an infant and he wanted her to go to sleep, he'd hold her on his lap, doing nothing to make her comfortable. After a while she found being in her crib a relief and would go right to sleep. Both my cousin and I thought that sounded a little unlikely.

3. Bear Claws

My Korean friend in Virginia sent me her Swiss friend so I could take him camping in the desert. First thing he noticed about me was that I didn't speak French or even German. First thing I noticed about him was that he had a funny little beard. The second thing I noticed was that he didn't speak English.

Then we were holding opposite ends of a tent that had ambitions to be a sail. Sand drove against us and huge drops of water stung our legs and faces as they flew sideways in the wind. Inside the tent, a bit later, first Patrice rose up into the air as the tent floor pushed under him, then I lost contact with the ground. We were on a see-saw made of air. We were both talking a lot. We may have been saying the same things. I don't know.

A week later we were walking up a steep mountainside in New Mexico's Jemez Mountains. A woman had told me about a hot spring up there. I couldn't figure out how to explain to Patrice in sign language what we were doing. But by that time I think he was pretty used to being surprised. There really wasn't any alternative to surprising him a lot, so it was convenient that he appeared to enjoy the repeated sense of astonishment as we made our way from one wonder to another.

And he was only slightly less prepared for all this than I was. I knew we were hiking toward a hot spring, but I had no idea what that really meant, never having seen one before. And then there it was, exhaling warm mist into the forest. We left our clothes on the ground and, each in his own world, slipped into the steaming pool.

After a while I stepped out on the rocks and made my way downhill to where a hot waterfall poured out of the pool. Standing under the cascade, I saw through the wavy sheet of water the mountainside dropping precipitously away below me, the next forested hill across the valley, and snow-capped ranges beyond. Taking a hot shower in that setting seemed so incongruous that I couldn't suppress a hilarious smile.

Warmed and massaged by the cascade, I stepped up onto an exposed rock and just stood for several minutes, reveling in the expansive view, the evergreen scent, the tingle of the brisk air. I usually feel suffocated in a hot bath and then chilled when I get out. But that wasn't happening. I felt like a sun radiating heat into the cold air. I was more comfortable than I could remember ever having been. Comfort verging on euphoria. The cool mountain breeze stroked me. It's crystalline, autumn prick didn't frighten me. I had plenty of warmth stored inside me. I felt safe.

It occurred to me that I could never reconstruct this experience, that it was a completely unsought-for, unrepeatable stumbling into paradise. The mere act of trying to set it up again would be enough to prevent its happening. Besides, the air would never be exactly this temperature again with just this amount of movement. The sound of the falling water, the fragrance would never be just as it was now.

At the end of the trip, we stopped at a Pueblo Indian jeweler's shop. Patrice said the name of his girlfriend and pointed to the case of earrings. He wanted some help picking out a present. I pointed to a few pair that looked nice. He shook his head and held up one finger. I pointed to my favorite pair. He pointed to his ear and then to me, so I put on the earrings for him to see how they looked. He grinned. I started to take them off but he shook his head and put up his hand like a traffic cop. He reached in his pocket, pulled out a necklace, and said, "Pour Madeleine." He had tricked me into choosing my own present.

Weeks later, Georgia mentioned to me that she knew something was shifting for me because I was wearing Bear

Claws. "Is that what they are?" You see, I hadn't known that before.

4. Dowsing Rods

"Are you waiting for the bus, honey?" inquired a pleasant-looking older woman. "It doesn't come until after midnight, you know." She glanced at her husband then back at me. The three of us chatted a bit. "This is no place for you to wait. It'll soon be dark and cold." And so it was decided that I should come spend the evening with them and then they would return me to the bus stop.

I was in Oregon for a series of job interviews. Some felt quite hopeful, but I wasn't certain I wanted to move again so soon. At any rate, it would be entertaining to spend some time with this friendly couple.

We rode in their van into a wooded area and stopped on a tiny dirt road. Without the headlights, the forest was quite dark by then. My two hosts had been telling me about dowsing rods. They had a large number of children, all grown now, some of whom could dowse and some of whom couldn't. You're born with the ability, they explained. You can't learn it any more than you could learn to see if you were born blind. I nodded and smiled politely. The whole concept sounded pretty weird to me.

But now we were stopping in the woods so they could demonstrate. At least, that's what I thought until the man held out the angle irons for me to hold. The time had come, I realized in a panic, for me to confess my skepticism. I just couldn't pretend to believe in this stuff, no matter how offended my guides might be. To my surprise, they responded to my disclaimer with indifference. "It doesn't matter if you believe in it, honey. You either do it or you don't. It doesn't make any difference what you think about it."

Well, as long as they didn't mind my mistrust of the thing, I didn't mind holding the irons and walking down the dark, forest road as they suggested. It just seemed sort of silly. But it was better than standing at the bus stop.

The two had not told me what "doing it" would look like, so I was in no danger of trying to duplicate the effect of a real dowser, assuming that such a person existed, which seemed unlikely to me.

Thirty or forty meters down the track, I lost my grip on the rods momentarily and reorganized them in my hands as I continued. Twenty or thirty meters more and the old man, who'd been following at a distance, called after me to turn back. I guessed he was disappointed at my performance. At the same point where the rods had slipped before, they did it again. The man, having closed some of the distance between us, asked me what was happening. "They slipped a little," I replied blandly.

"Hm. Did that on the way out, too, didn't they?" Goodness, he wasn't going to try to make something of this, was he? I just lost my grip for a minute and the rods crossed in front of me. That's all. "Why don't you take a look around, see where you are," the stooped old man suggested. Seemed a silly idea to me. Of course I knew where I was. In the middle of the woods. But, to humor him, and perhaps partly because he had aroused my curiosity ever so slightly, I stepped to the side of the road. Dimly, I could make out the black trunks of trees silhouetted against something brighter. A pond. Well, I'll be. I hadn't noticed a body of water off among the trees. But I hoped he wasn't going to try to convince me that it had anything to do with my slipping angle irons.

"Take a look to the other side," he suggested. So, I did. No pond over there. But then, looking down at my feet, I saw the opening of a culvert. This was the outlet of the pond. There was a culvert right under this part of the road, just where I lost control of the rods.

I'd have to give this some thought. I could suggest no mechanism to explain the phenomenon called dowsing. But neither could I offer an alternative explanation for my slipping rods. As a rule, I simply kept away from things I couldn't explain. That way I could be done with it by saying they didn't exist.

Hm, the couple hadn't told me what might happen to the rods if I were a "dowser." In fact, that was good, not because I didn't know what to fake but because I didn't know what to block. Surely, I'd have prevented having to face an inexplicable phenomenon in my own hands. I could have continued then to think of my hosts as cranks who had talked themselves into believing a fairy tale. But now I couldn't do that. I hadn't seen someone else counterfeit a reaction. I'd experienced myself something I'd never seen or heard described.

The experience in the Oregon woods left me in a bind. I could either pretend that it hadn't happened or I could accept the existence of something for which I had no explanation. At first disquieting, the latter possibility began gradually to feel kind of exciting.

5. Death and Children

A small slug oozed up a leaf at the corner of my clipboard and then stretched to its full centimeter's length to reach another leaf, its tail making the crossing on a mucus bridge. The sun glinted for a second on the ephemeral engineering feat. The slug's side opened and an exchange occurred between the moist creature and the atmosphere; some of the air became part of the slug's body. In fact, where did the slug end and the air begin? Despite the definitional problem, how delicate, how perfect seemed this temporary organization of particles into a slug.

My first day on the new job had gone well. I had met teachers from Indian schools all over the country. I'd be training them in techniques of science instruction during the next week and would be in touch with them through visits, phone calls and a newsletter throughout the coming year—except for the previous night's dinner companion. He had told me about his recent, painful divorce, a tremendously difficult first year at a remote school in Montana, and his dream of going to Alaska.

A few hours later, awakened from a hard sleep, I heard the words but could not at first take in the meaning, "Lee just died."

The next day, watching the slug, I still couldn't accept it as a good biologist would, as part of the cycle of nutrients through the environment, part of life. It seemed all wrong. There must have been a cosmic screw-up. He was so sad, so unsettled. And he never got to see Alaska.

In conversation with another teacher that day, I mentioned my distress about Lee's death. Ben offered some comfort by telling me that he and Lee had spent the late evening together laughing so hard that his stomach still hurt. The last thing Lee said as they walked back to the dorm, the foothills of the Rockies looming behind it, was, "Isn't it beautiful here?" Then he went up to his room to work on his first assignment. "He died leaning over his 'wish list,'" Ben said with a slight wrinkling around the eyes that matured into a smile as he added, "There was nothing on it. Maybe all he wanted was to die in that moment when he was happy."

Ben went on to remind me of something Lee had said during a conversation the three of us had had the previous day. He had described an exercise he liked to do with his students. He took them all to a creek and set each of them out of sight of the others by the stream. He let them sit there for twenty or thirty minutes with the instructions to notice every sensation they could, every sound, smell, color, movement. Ben said he got up early this morning, went outside, and did that in memory of Lee and as an exercise in being alive. I took the next opportunity to do it myself and felt better.

Chief Seathl of the Duamish Indians said, "The air is precious to the red man, for all things share the same breath." I looked for the slug but couldn't find it. Chief Seathl also said, "You must teach your children that the ground beneath their feet is the ashes of our grandfathers. So that they will respect the land, tell your children that the earth is rich with the lives of our kin." I had hoped that people might gain a deeper ecological understanding at this workshop. At least one person was, me.

I watched dramatic cloud formations that evening, impossibly rich blue. A hole broke in the turbulent sky dome, and the day's last sunlight funneled through, giving sudden distinction to a small disc of otherwise nondescript prairie. My eyes took in the ranges of mountains to the west, each a flat, misty replica of the range before it. Could Alaska be more beautiful?

Mary is a young Menominee woman who at the age of three was adopted by friends of mine, when her grandmother on the reservation in Wisconsin felt she could no longer protect Mary from her violent father.

Her adopted father has been studying Hopewell Indian sites in Ohio. There is a particular mound that interests him. The mound itself is in the shape of an eagle. Buried in the mound were two metal objects, a beaver and a disc like the sun or the moon. For months Cliff tried to find a story which involved an eagle, a beaver, and the sun or the moon. Eventually he set the question aside and went on to other things.

A few years later, Mary asked her dad if he was still looking for a story. She knew one.

> *There was a time when the sun disappeared. The animals gathered to talk about the problem. Finally the eagle volunteered to go search for the sun. After flying many miles, he found the sun caught in an enormous spider's web. The eagle knew that he could not release the sun from the web because his feathers would burn if he flew close. So, he returned to the other animals and told them what he had found. Each animal had a good reason not to go retrieve the sun. Finally the beaver—which was not the beaver we know today, but a scrawny animal with a thin coat and a spindly tail—the beaver said that since he didn't have much to lose he would go try to release the sun. So, the eagle carried him to the great web where the sun was caught. Despite the searing heat, the beaver chewed through the strands of the web until the sun was freed. The eagle, taking pity on the beaver, carried him back home where the Great Spirit, pleased by his bravery, rewarded him with the finest coat and widest tail of all the animals.*

When Cliff asked Mary where she had heard the story, she said in school. But after interviewing each of Mary's teachers, Cliff had turned up no one who recognized the story.

That first week I worked for the professional society of American Indian scientists, when I found that among the participants of the teacher-training workshop were two

Menominee women, I made a point of sitting with them at a meal. We were eating dessert before I got up my courage and asked if they would listen to a story I had heard. When I finished, Charlene, the older of the women, looked at me blankly. I was embarrassed. She'd never heard this story; my hunch had been wrong.

No, I suddenly thought in terror, she *does* know it and I'm not supposed to! We sat in silence for several long minutes.

"Actually," said Charlene to my enormous relief, "the eagle dropped the beaver in the water when they got back, to help soothe his burns. That's where the beaver has lived ever since." She went on to say that the Great Spirit gave him not only a fine, thick coat and a special tail but also yellow teeth, the color of the sun, to remind everyone that he was the one who had freed the sun. She also said that before the eagle went in search of the sun, many other animals had tried and failed.

Weeks later I realized that Charlene's silence had been her politely waiting for me to finish the story. Since she knew I hadn't completed it, she gave me a good long time to gather my thoughts and my words.

I'd leave it to Cliff to work out the archeological significance. I was beside myself with excitement about having found this connection between Mary's story and her Menominee heritage. Charlene said that this story was one of the two most often told to children by their grandmothers. Charlene declined to tell me the other. I didn't need to know it. I hoped, though, that it would come back to Mary. If she remembered this one from when she was three, she'd probably remember the other one eventually.

Also during that first week-long workshop, we went on several field trips. One day we tracked alpine mammals. Another day we visited the American Indian Hall of the

Denver Museum of Natural History.

Joseph walked next to me through the museum hall for several minutes before he said, "There are some mistakes in this exhibit." I asked him what he'd noticed and suggested he tell our guide so that the errors could be corrected. In fact, the man leading the group had asked them to share any thoughts or concerns with him. Having people from so many different tribes present at the exhibit was a real asset for the museum. "There's something wrong with the Hupa display," Joseph continued. "The man holding the white deer skin never kneels." I looked into the case. It depicted the White Deer Skin Dance. I asked Joseph if he did that dance. The story which emerged from that simple question was to influence the rest of my life.

Joseph was a bright kid. He didn't tell me this. He said that someone had picked him out while he was in school and helped him make it through the ordeal of high school and into college. He received an advanced degree, got a well-paid job in Los Angeles, married, had two kids and lived in a nice house. One day he woke up, asked, "Whose life am I living?" and walked away from all of it: job, family, house, security. He wandered for months, living on the streets. Throughout this time he had the sense that there was something he needed to do, but he didn't know what it was. Eventually he found himself back at the Hupa Reservation although he hadn't consciously intended to go there. He started hanging out with the men who do the White Deer Skin Dance, a dance of world renewal. He became absorbed in the dance and quickly realized that it was what had drawn him away from L.A. and through the months. Focussed on the dance and without effort, Joseph started a new life, *his* life. Things began to fall together. He became the manager of the local radio station and instituted Hupa-language programming. He did work with the schools. He was reunited with his family. He came to the teacher training workshop in Colorado because he figured someone from Hupa should go and none of the teachers seemed interested.

This was my first encounter with a hero's journey. I had no model or instruction for this sort of search in my past, and Joseph's path was completely contrary to the cerebral approach I had been taught all my life. I was thrilled by his story. You mean there are other ways to do things besides figuring out what you should do, acquiring the skills to do it, and then doing it? You mean you could float in the mystery, stop struggling to go somewhere, and leave yourself open to the gentle tug of a distant, unknown magnet? What would that be like, I wondered? Was there a magnet pulling me right now perhaps, with a force too small for me to sense while I was busy thrashing about? Oh, probably not. These things probably happen only to Indians or Buddhist monks.

Our week of work done, we relaxed in the dorm lobby on the last evening, drinking ginger ale, laughing, gently letting down the barriers that remained between us.

We talked about death. It was on our minds. It was very nearly the first experience we had shared, and it was something we all faced. One of the Menominee women said that she had been very confused about what to do when the group had been called together in the middle of the night to learn of Lee's death. "There were prayers to be said, things to do. But a man is supposed to say those prayers. But there are no Menominee men here." As soon as that meeting had ended, Charlene and the other Menominee woman had gone to their room, burned the right herbs, and said the right prayers. If there were no men in the room, then it was all right for a woman to do those things. An older man, taciturn all week, said with what might have been a smile, "In my tribe, it's the women who must say the prayers." He, too, had sought the solitude of his room that night, to make his saying of the prayers acceptable. Knowing smiles reflected around the group.

I had gotten some balloons and refreshments for the children who were with us. When they fell asleep, the adults continued playing with the balloons. A favorite game was a relay race in which pairs of people carried balloons between them. Another was a sort of group juggling, using only our feet as we sat in a ring on the floor.

The night passed in comfortable alternation of dance improvisation (often with balloons), ancient games from various tribes, tumbling, and soul-searching discussion. We shared the liberating effect of the summer night air.

We had made it. We could talk about death and act like children.

It was odd how I'd gotten that job. I answered ads, dressed properly for interviews, asked intelligent questions. But that's not how I got the job. That's how I spent several months being miserable. Then one day I decided, this is a drag. I'm going to take a break, do something interesting. I'd seen a notice on a bulletin board somewhere asking for volunteers to help judge science fairs on Indian reservations. I'd never met an Indian person and never been to a science fair. It would be interesting.

Completely relaxed because I was now on vacation from my job search, I called the phone number from the bulletin board. An hour later, the Klamath woman I'd been talking with about everything under the sun—science fairs first, of course—suddenly asked, "You don't want a job, do you? I mean a real one, for money, not volunteer. It would be mostly training teachers and then developing other projects to promote science education in Indian schools."

I couldn't believe it. I'd heard, of course, that you get what you need when you learn to let go. But I'd never imagined it could happen so fast. How long had it been? Ten minutes to find the phone number and an hour in conversation. So much for that vacation.

6. Journeys

I got in the habit of sitting down in my big chair and shutting my eyes whenever I got an urge to. Usually a guide appeared and took me on an inner journey. And usually it took me a while to recognize the guide.

One time it was a retarded man. He led me up a steep mountain and then sliced himself in two by jumping on the sharp mountaintop. His two halves curled away into a fantastic dance in the air. After a while, they slid up opposite sides of the mountain and rejoined. The man couldn't speak, but he split and danced again, apparently to demonstrate how much fun it was. Disappointed that I didn't try the trick myself, he quickly divided and mended a couple more times to make it clear how easy and painless it was. Finally losing patience with my cautiousness, he started pushing on my head, hoping to force me to split. I didn't like the pressure and pushed back. But, despite my resistance, one half of me suddenly slid down one side of the mountain and one half down the other. The two pieces of myself whirled and somersaulted, floated up and hurtled down in an ecstatic dance. After reuniting my halves, I tried a couple more splits just to make sure I could do it. No pain, no fear lingered. Pure joy.

Lots of these inner trips seemed to be at least in part about letting go of resistance and about accepting guidance from unexpected quarters. On another occasion in my big chair, I found myself in a sleazy, poorly-lit neighborhood. I was standing behind some shabby, wooden tenements and could feel filth and crime in the air. A hooker wearing a tight dress and red, high-heeled shoes beckoned for me to follow her. I ignored her distracting gesture. I was waiting for my guide. The hooker had started up a wooden stairway on the back of one of the dingy apartment buildings. She turned and looked over her shoulder at me. Oh, I get it. *You're* my guide. Of course. Always what I least expect. And I followed her up the rickety stairs to a dark, smokey room full of fat men.

Then the phone rang and I opened my eyes. I never did find out what that hooker had to teach me.

When I thought about who my guides were, where they came from, I pictured them as the disowned parts of myself, the parts which had been prevented from speaking their message. Mine was a psychological interpretation. An acquaintance surprised me by referring to these guides as God's voice. Initially put off by the religious language, I later thought about it again and realized we both used metaphor to speak about the phenomenon. Hers located the source of insight outside and mine inside. But if you look again, the only difference in our explanations dissolves. She spoke of "that of God in everyone" and "the Inner Light." So, for her, God wasn't just outside but was also a part of a person. And when I thought of these guides, these disowned personality parts, I saw them as bearers of gifts. They brought things I greatly needed, things which I felt I didn't have. Pleasantly, the dichotomy between internal and external began to evaporate. My personality parts seemed to bring me wisdom from outside myself. And my friend's "voice of God" could be part of me.

True, I had developed a severe allergy to religious, especially Christian, language. But for the first time, I recognized that such words might be used to refer to things I acknowledged with different language. I'd stick to my own, but perhaps I could begin to hear what other people were talking about when they used the allergenic words like God, Holy Ghost, and so on. If I could translate "God led me here" quickly enough to "the deepest part of me knew to come here," I might be able to listen without nausea.

One day I found myself at the base of a stone tower, part of a castle. I stood around waiting for someone to turn up. No one came. A stone stairway inside the tower seemed the obvious place to go. Perhaps the stair itself was my guide this time. I started up. For once I knew immediately what I would do on this trip, or what I would have the opportunity to do. I was not surprised when the stairway ended at an open window in the top of the tower. I stood on the ledge for a few moments, reminding myself that this was just a daydream so I couldn't actually get hurt, and then I jumped.

In fact, I seemed to need to do this particular journey a number of times. Once I floated gently to the green lawn at the bottom of the tower. Another time, far from floating, I plummeted down past the tower into a hole in the ground. Soon, it became so dark that I could no longer see the rocky walls I was whizzing past. Eventually I shot out the end of a tunnel and banged gracelessly down a slope, tearing my coat as I went. But that was only the beginning of that day's trip, which evolved into a series of dramatic metamorphoses. I became a flower, was plucked, and floated down a river. I was at various times a homeless old woman, a piece of pink tissue squashed under a boot heel, and a feather drifting in a breeze.

After some weeks, the jumping journeys tapered off, and I began having different sorts of experiences in my big chair. And almost always, as soon as I "figured out" what it was about, something would shift to make it clear that that was not at all what it was about. I never got over the habit of trying to interpret while these things were happening, but I stopped being surprised that I was almost always wrong.

Once I sat, eyes closed, waiting for some unlikely guide to appear in some equally unlikely setting. But no fantastic landscape opened up before my mind's eye, no vast desert or deep chasm, no damp dungeon or squalid hut. And no guide approached me. I just sat there.

Then I became aware of two hands on my head, but I still couldn't see anything. Gradually the hands started to pull the two sides of my head in opposite directions. My skull made a wrenching noise and split open. My left eye dangled over my left shoulder and my right eye wobbled in its half of my head over my right shoulder. But the hands didn't stop. They kept pulling until my neck split, my sternum cracked with a jolting pop, and my torso tore into two mushy halves. The hands then placed a scrap of lumber down my center, bracing one edge against my backbone, and pushed and kneaded my tissues into the old board. I was getting some reinforcement. How peculiar. (By this time, I was long past expecting or experiencing any pain during such operations.) It felt like being armored for war, but from the inside, and I wasn't planning on going to war. Somehow, though, it felt good to get strengthened that way, to feel my tissues knitting into the wood as the hands reunited my two halves.

7. The Mouse

The mice were beginning to get to me. Every morning I cleaned the droppings off the sink counter and washed the urine off the spoon before eating breakfast. I found shreds of paper fluffed behind my sweaters in the dresser. I learned quickly to put all food in cans or in the fridge. But then mice consider your dried-weed bouquet food. So, it took several re-definitions before I was fairly certain I wasn't feeding them. But warm shelter is also important as the days become cold and short, and I couldn't help but offer free housing, what with the holes in my floor and the cozy nesting boxes that I had previously thought of as dresser drawers.

One morning after a particularly long session with the kitchen utensils, I marched downtown to the hardware store and bought mouse traps. That night, I woke from a deep sleep to the sound of a decisive snap. Yuck. Well, it was quick. Back to sleep. But as I drifted in that direction, I heard a rattling on the other side of the bedroom wall. Oh my god, it's alive. Not for long, I'm sure. But the rattling and scratching continued, peaking in a ferocious crashing and banging against the wall by my head. Then it stopped. Death throes, I thought. Gees, that was horrible. I slipped off to sleep.

The dream about the prisoner gradually blended with the chains rattling by my head. No, not chains. It was the mouse still thrashing around attached to the trap. Sickness welled up in my belly. Fatigue pulled at my mind. Sleep. It'll die soon. Sleep. Please die. How could I be saying that? Why did I set that trap?

But sleep did free me from the thumping and rattling of the dying mouse. Until a particularly bad crash, now down by my feet, brought me again into a fuzzy, nightmarish consciousness. How could it live so long? I can't stand it. I dragged my complaining, sleep-starved body out of bed and lurched into the main room. The lamp illuminated a small grey mouse caught across the pelvis by the metal bar. It had dragged the wooden, spring-loaded trap all the way across the room from under the stove to under the big western window. As I approached, it flopped again, the trap landing on top of it this time.

Fast. I had to kill it fast. I should have gotten up earlier. I shouldn't have let it struggle this long. I heard it and didn't do anything. Well, now I would do it right. I picked up the trap gingerly by its edges and carried it out into the cold, starry night. The flat stones of the path burned cold against my bare feet.

Now, this had to be done right. I wouldn't want to miss or hit too timidly and then have to do it again. No, perhaps not this rock. Too irregular. A target that small could end up in a crevice and not get smashed. The skull. That would be best. Smash its skull. Jesus! Am I doing this? My hand is shaking. Now don't hold back out of some sentimental desire to be gentle. Smash it. Hit it hard. End the misery. I didn't hold back. The rock bashed the trap, making it spring up and rattle like a snake. But the mouse still struggled. I hadn't done it right. My eyes were too blind, my hand too shaky, my aim too imprecise. Releasing the mouse from the trap, I laid its mangled, twitching little body on a flat stone. Its fur was so soft I couldn't feel it.

The rock splattered its entire body this time. Drops of the mouse stuck to my toes. Frantic, I ran up the hillside, scraping the pink tissue off in the dry grass. A cactus against my ankle reminded me to make a slower, more studied retreat. Rock, trap, and squashed mouseparts flung into the draw, I went back inside to pull cactus prickles and wash and wash my hands and feet. It took a long time to get the blood off my foot. Or to be sure it was gone. You can't be too sure.

Afterward, I lay a long time shivering between the cold sheets. It was awfully cold for October.

8. Hummingbirds

The broad-tailed hummers were returning. I'd noticed them, mostly the males' metallic whirring. That meant it was a year since I'd left Vance or Vance had left me, whichever way you wanted to look at it.

I bought a hummingbird feeder. A friend had told me how

to do this. You hang it quite a distance from your house so the birds can get used to it without you nearby. Then over a period of a week or so you move it gradually closer to your house and eventually hang it by your window.

The hillside behind my cabin hosted all kinds of wonderful plants: prickly pear cactus, lupines, yuccas, poppies, grasses, and a number of small herbs you notice only in early spring when in a reproductive frenzy before the scorch they send up their fuzzy purple goblets or white snowflakes or whatever. But there was nothing on which I could hang a hummingbird feeder. Oh, there were trees in the draw cutting straight up the hill to the tiny but dependable spring. But what with their being only a few meters tall and standing in the bottom of the little gully, they didn't offer any elevation. Their crowns made only a slight lump in the landscape running down the hillside right past the corner of the cabin. The draw was the main thing that made this spot magical, but it wasn't a place to hang a hummingbird feeder.

I finally decided on the clothesline pole. Hanging the feeder there started me smiling, then giggling. The first time I'd done laundry in Colorado, I'd hung it on that clothesline. As I started back toward the cabin, I brushed against the cotton sheet I'd hung up first. It was dry. So was the shirt hanging next to it. So, is this how you do laundry in Colorado? You hang things up, then turn around and take them down, fold them, and put them in your bureau? Clothes could hang out for days in Virginia just thinking about getting dry but never quite getting the gumption to do it. From that day on, laundry was my favorite joke. I told eastern friends about it. They didn't believe me. I told them it was so dry in Colorado that a short person had trouble washing his hair in the shower. The water evaporated before it reached his head. They didn't believe that either.

The clothes pole was only four meters from the big

window. Actually, the window wasn't that big, but since it filled the entire western wall of my main room, it was the biggest feature of the little frame structure. And since it looked out on the hillside and its draw full of wild plum, chokecherry and hawthorn, and since the trickle of water and the trees drew butterflies and deer and coyotes and lazuli buntings and western tanagers, the window was the most important part of the cabin. More important than the four hundred square feet of floor space (although being cozy was part of its charm).

I knew the feeder was too close to the cabin for its first day, but there wasn't much choice and, anyway, I had conveniently started doubting the authority of my friend. Why would the hummers be more frightened of the feeder on the clothes pole than on a tree? Well, I suppose they might be, but never mind.

Five minutes later I asked myself why a bird would be less frightened of a feeder on a pole four meters from a cabin than a feeder hanging from the eaves of that cabin. I went outside, retrieved the artificial nectary from the clothesline and carried it the few steps to the hook I had already screwed into the beam just over the window—to be ready for the big move a week later, you know.

As I untangled the cord, I thought about the rest of what my friend had told me, the part about the weeks of patient waiting several meters away from the feeder, moving gradually closer each day as the birds became accustomed to your presence. He said you could eventually stand right by the feeder and even raise your hand and stroke the belly of a hungry hummingbird as it dined. I could tell I wasn't going to have the patience for that project. Look at me so far. Five minutes and I was already hanging the feeder by my window.

As I raised it toward the hook, a little helicopter buzzed over my left shoulder and began to drink. I didn't know what to do. The feeder wasn't even fastened to the cabin yet. What the heck. My friend was obviously misinformed. I moved my left hand slowly down under the blurred bird, still holding the feeder in my right. My huge fingers rose slowly, so did the hummer. So much for the Lesson in Patience. Was he just rising of his own accord, avoiding my impinging hand, or was I lifting him? Ever so slowly—but don't be too long; he'll get full and leave—I tilted my head down to bird level. There he was, breast feathers dented onto my enormous knuckles. But my skin was not sensitive enough to feel the brush of these unimaginably soft feathers, nor were the scales of my hand calibrated finely enough to register the weight of this ethereal being. I concluded laughingly on the basis of the zero readings on all my instruments that a hummingbird has no physical existence but is only a spirit or perhaps an illusion. Well, OK, or I might be trying to weigh an electron on a truck scale.

It wasn't really that I didn't want to finish the dishes. It was just that I knew it was time to head up the draw. No particular sound or scent drew me, not that I was conscious of. Nevertheless, there was a strong pull. I was actually enjoying the warm sudsy water and the satisfaction of the pile of clean dishes accumulating in the drainer. So, I must say again that it wasn't avoidance but something positive, a magnetism rather than a repulsion. Now, there are times when I do resist doing dishes and will find any excuse, even vacuuming, to keep my hands out of the sink; but this wasn't one of them, so, we'll leave that.

A draw. And that it is, an alluring cleft in the hillside, too shallow to be called a canyon or even a ravine, but too seductive to be ignored a moment longer. So, leaving the water in the sink and the door wide open, I stepped over the fence—there are certain advantages to long legs—and ducked into the thicket—and certain disadvantages, I should add.

Just like the deer who disappear into these bushes many times a day, within seconds I was in a different world from the sunny, cactus-spotted slope behind my cabin. Now the sounds did draw me. Suddenly there was a confusion of bird song. It had been too long since last spring for me to remember which tune came from which species, but they were all familiar. I tunneled on under the scratching twigs and tangled vines. Even though I knew from having crawled in here before that the area just above the trickle of water that always flowed was no more free of vegetation than anywhere else in the thicket, I headed there anyway. Squatting with my feet in the water and my head in a chokecherry—at least it wasn't a hawthorn—I listened. Then just above my head there was a flurry of feathers. Stuck as I was, I couldn't really move my head to get a good view. But from the corner of my eye as I tilted my head sideways, I did see a great commotion involving two sparrow-sized birds. Mating. It must be. All this flapping and chirping. It didn't seem like a territorial squabble. When one of the birds flew a couple feet up the draw, I saw through a convenient series of small gaps between branches that it was a pine siskin.

As I crawled farther uphill, each inch dearly won by weaving through the dense confusion of woody plants, I became aware of the nearly constant metallic whirring of the male hummingbirds darting just a few feet above me and my green cover. From time to time, I caught a glimpse of one on a bare branch. Once, twisting awkwardly around to get a look at a startling orange object I'd barely seen flit through the branches above me, I saw, completely by chance, a female hummer plucking insects from a spider's web or else collecting silk to line its nest. I watched it a long time. Something made me think it was feeding. Oh, yes, occasionally it did a bit of fly-catching from a twig. Then it visited the web again, and, perhaps significantly, did not go away between visits.

Eventually I did catch up with the orange splash, a Bullock's oriole. It was joined shortly by a soft yellow female, and then there was more fluttering and twittering.

In this shady, sheltered spot grew a completely different set of plants from those on the exposed hillside to either side. White violets and bluebells bloomed on the muddy slope beneath the last of the wild plum blossoms and the profuse white cylinders of chokecherry flowers. The hawthorns, anything but inconspicuous despite their unopened buds, drew my acute attention with their two-inch thorns.

Still only a few meters from my cabin, but completely concealed from it, I made my way through the dump of old bottles and rusted tins. A bedspring nearly perfectly camouflaged by vines presented the trickiest obstacle to my progress. As I puzzled over how to extricate my left ankle from the rusted wire, I noticed the wash tub. It had a spigot near its bottom. I'd never before met a spigotted wash tub. It intrigued me. As I became able, I made my way over to the relic. Under its influence, suddenly all the debris came alive for me and spoke of the humans who had used and discarded these objects at the beginning of the century. Their clothes got dirty, just as mine were right now, and they washed them in this tub and then drained the stained water out the spigot. Somehow, this seemed the most intimate thing I could know about a person. I was almost embarrassed to be seeing the refuse of these dead people, strangers who weren't even there to distract my gaze from their secret trash. But they were no longer strangers, for I had discovered their hidden truth: their clothes got dirty, just like mine.

Overcome with something like shyness, I climbed out of the draw and found a perch on a rock. The soft, early-summer air caressed me. Then, focussing my eyes where they had been resting for some time, I looked down into the thicket where a buck lay dozing. He was no more than three meters below my dangling feet and utterly relaxed. Feeling again that I had stumbled into someone's private affairs, I slid back on my stone and walked quietly down the hill.

As the summer hummed on, activity around the feeder was intense. For a few days early on, some rufous hummingbirds terrorized the regulars, the broad-tails. But they moved on, leaving the locals to their routine. Near the end of the season, the next generation flooded out into the world and made space around the feeder an air traffic controller's nightmare.

Late in the summer, my cabin door and windows gasping open in the 100-degree heat, I sat writing at my desk when a hummingbird whirred into the tiny room. A jeweled male, flashing his scarlet throat in the relentless sunbeams. He was the second such visitor I'd had that summer. I thought it was great until I realized that he didn't know how to get out. Give him time. There are lots of holes in this little cabin, some intentional and others the product of 80 years of wind and rodents on the thin-walled structure. He'll get out. But he didn't. Thinking back to the visit of the female hummer a few weeks earlier, I picked up a bandanna and sidled over to the shelf where he sat exhausted after his increasingly frantic attempts at escape. That was where the female had retired, too, and where I had slipped a handkerchief over her and carried her outside. (Is she really in my hand? I don't feel anything but the hanky.) And released her. (My gosh, she really *was* in my hand; there she goes.)

But the male was fluttering up against the ceiling before I got half-way across the 15-foot-wide room. He finally dropped to a log rafter and sat open-beaked, panting. Perhaps I could catch him up there.

I was barely atop the chair, though, when he flew off against the south wall. Just a bit lower, I was pleading, and you'll be out the door. Gees, I'm only frightening you. This is horrible. I forced myself to return to my work, pretending not to notice the tiny bird alternately flinging itself against walls and sitting exhausted on a rafter. It made no more low-altitude forays into window and door level. From time to time its terror was too much for me and I leapt up, determined to catch it and carry it outside. But my attempts at rescue only exacerbated its panic. By evening, I was nearly in tears and beginning to feel trapped myself in the stifling wooden cabin.

My eyes wandered toward the small fabric picture hanging on the east wall. In it, a blue stream flowed from distant mountains into a green meadow where people picked enormous carrots and milked fat cows. Suddenly I knew why I had impulsively bought the applique from an Argentinean man. It was the peaceful meadow to which I'd always longed to return ever since my childhood dream. It was a place to rest safely.

My sweaty back sticking to my chair—in that arid climate, it's only a part of you that isn't exposed to the dry air that ever feels wet, even in the height of summer—I tilted my head back to watch the hummer's latest feeble flight. To my astonishment, he dipped, perhaps from fatigue, lower than usual and sailed out the east window. It was over.

Well, I mused later, it was over for me, but how about the hummingbird? I'd seen from my observation of the feeder how frequently these tiny creatures ate. How near the edge did they live? This little guy had not only missed nearly an entire feeding day, but had also expended enormous amounts of energy in his attempts to escape. He was obviously depleted by the time he got out, his flights having become shorter, less frequent and markedly less energetic. How quickly could he re-stock his energy supplies? Was there time before nightfall? If not, could he last through the night? How damaged was he? Could a creature survive that much deprivation? Or would this fragile little bird die?

There. I had finally asked the question. Was it going to die tonight?

9. Fawns

One June morning, at the beginning of that second year in the cabin, I was eating a bowl of rice and beans out back, looking up at the hillside, still lush with spring lupines. A deer emerged from the draw and waded gracefully through the green ocean, just a few meters up the hill from where I sat on the little wooden deck next to the cabin. I'd seen this doe quite a bit recently, mostly near the draw. I knew it was the same one by the orange tag numbered 168 hanging from her ear. Someone must be studying the large deer population in the area.

Momentarily caught up in the watery imagery, I didn't think to wonder at the wake behind the moving doe. But wait. Deer don't really create a wake in grass the way a beaver does in a pond. Why *was* that grass behind her swaying? Just then the doe stepped onto a rocky patch of ground and two fawns emerged from the grass behind her. In a moment they were back among the tall stems and leaves, the fawns hidden again from view.

From time to time in the following weeks, I saw the trio out on the hillside. The fawns began exploring farther and farther from their mother, checking in every so often to nurse and feel her comforting presence. Occasionally one made an almost human-sounding cry which brought the doe to its side.

One morning as I sat on the back deck scanning the hillside for activity, a beautiful coyote ambled into view from my left. I loved watching the coyotes out back. They were so soft, such wonderful dry colors, and their movements betrayed such an appealing combination of indifference, agility, playfulness, and toughness. Suddenly its casual posture stiffened, it picked up speed, and darted directly into the draw at my right.

A scream from the thicket froze my hand as it reached for a spoonful of mashed potatoes. Another scream followed. Number 168 tore across the dry hillside at the right of the draw and dived into the thicket.

Silence clutched the hill. My hand was still poised over my bowl. I could hardly breathe. It must be too late. The fawn was already dead. Mom was too late.

Then another shriek shattered the brittle air. I could see nothing of the drama in the draw. The brush was too thick. But neither coyote, fawn, nor doe appeared at the edges of the thicket. They all must still be in the little ravine. I should be going to work, but I sat paralysed holding my spoon and my breath.

Suddenly a desperate crying commenced, different from the earlier, alarmed screams. I imagined the fawn struggling for its life, the doe... What would she be doing? Kicking her sharp hooves at the coyote? I didn't know what was really happening. But I wanted it to stop. Why did the beautiful coyote have to eat the beautiful fawn? Why were we caught in this paradox of life having to feed on itself? I didn't want it to be that way. And I just couldn't think of it as the recycling and reorganizing of raw material that allows life to evolve ever-changing forms.

The crying stopped. At last it was over. But my spoon still hung over my bowl. I couldn't move. The fawn was dead.

Then another shriek and more agonized crying. I found myself wishing only for the end, no longer for the fawn to appear bolting up the far side of the draw, the coyote dragging off in the other direction. If only the crying would stop. If only the fawn would die.

I don't know how many times the crying stopped—leaving

me afraid to hope but hoping none-the-less that the dying was over—only to start again with a shrillness and a strength that at once encouraged and terrified me that the fawn might survive even longer.

At last there was a silence that was longer than the others. Yes, it was definitely longer. Minutes and minutes. Surely this is it, the end. I waited, aching arm still clutching my empty spoon. Nothing happened. Not a sound, not a movement spoke of the events in the draw.

At last, a couple hours after I should have been at work, the coyote, as beautiful as ever in its desert-colored coat, trotted up the south side of the draw and headed casually uphill.

The following day, I ate my breakfast in heavy silence out back. The draw, the hillside seemed empty and lifeless. I struggled with grief and the knowledge that this is the way the world works. This is the way *I* work. Why, I was eating soup right now that was made of dead clams. Someone had killed the clams, not to mention the celery and onions and potatoes, for me to eat—so I could live. Life feeds on itself, like that serpent I'd seen in a print somewhere. These thoughts, however, did nothing to fill the emptiness I felt. Not even the clam chowder was doing that. But the sadness I felt was not about nature devouring itself. I didn't know what it was about.

Then, out of the corner of an eye, I caught a movement. Number 168 climbed out of the draw. A single fawn followed her. Grief swept through me like a sickness. I didn't like this. It barely got born before it got killed. It wasn't fair. I didn't care about the cycling of nutrients and flow of energy. I didn't care that Number 168 still had the other fawn. I hated this.

Then, the second fawn appeared from the draw, following its mother and sibling.

Involuntarily, I stood up. Definitely two fawns. No mistake. Number 168. Yes, it was the same doe and her *two* fawns. How...? What happened yesterday? What was...? The crying. It seemed so desperate. Is the fawn walking OK? Yes. Yes. It is. I can't see anything wrong with it. At least from this distance. In fact, I don't know which one was attacked yesterday. Perhaps both. But their movements seem fluid, normal. Neither of them is limping. The fawns are alive.

It had been difficult to explain why I'd arrived so late for work the previous day. It was harder the second day, but I didn't mind. I just had to watch those fawns, first to make sure they were really all right and then simply to enjoy the overwhelming ordinariness of it all. This is it. They're walking. They're eating. They're licking their fur. They're touching each other and then separating. They're stepping on brown plants. Isn't this great? They're stepping on plants.

10. The Wind Rivers

I stopped abruptly to listen, both legs and one sleeve tangled in the brush. That didn't matter. Listen. Not for a bear, although those were shiny bear droppings, fresh, not fifty meters back toward the lake shore. Not to the beaver gliding at the vertex of its own V on the lake surface. Not to the intermittent whisper of wind in the spruce and fir trees crowded around most of the lake and blanketing much of the mountainside, all but the steepest sections and the parts covered with scree. A gray jay squawked. But that was not what I attended to right then. Nor the twig which broke loose from the threads of my pant leg and whisked along the fabric, thwacking my other leg as it sprang into its resting position.

What caught my attention there among the bushes was the jabbering in my own head. It was shocking. At least three voices. They told me I'd set up my tent in the wrong place. The peninsula was too windy. They asked with irritation why I had chosen this route through all the brush. They asked patronizingly if I wouldn't prefer to walk around the other side of the lake where there were bare rocks near the shore. They asked ever so solicitously if I had read the compass correctly. Had I adjusted for the declination at this location? They asked why I stayed two nights at the same spot instead of maximizing my time in Wyoming by moving my campsite each day. "You aren't going to see much if you don't keep moving." Then: Was the Wind River Range perhaps too wild for me to be exploring alone?

That was it! *Alone* was what I wanted to be! "Who invited you? And I'm not here to see the whole range, to collect points in the game of who's been on the most mountains. I'm here to..." I stopped, annoyed that I was being sucked in by the critical questions. I was getting defensive. Explaining, justifying. It was a sickeningly familiar feeling. "You guys aren't invited!" I yelled. "Now, get out of here and don't come back!"

It was an enormous relief to feel that worried, critical presence leave. But it was shocking to realize that it had taken four days of solitude for me to notice that those voices were with me, correcting, testing, asking for justification constantly. In fact, my automatic explanations to them made me realize I'd been answering their questions not for days but for years. I didn't do anything without a good reason. I had to be able to articulate why I did everything I did. And reasons were the only acceptable justification, not hunches or feelings. A tongue of fury flared up from me, there on the mountain. I pictured it like the flaming gas which is vented from petroleum plants. I guess that wheedling, sarcastic mental station—the one I'd put off the air simply by noticing it—wasn't the only one which had been playing, probably 24 hours a day, in my head. Here was another talk show with three patronizing voices checking up on everything I did, every decision I made, seeing whether I did it right. What an idea! As if there is always one clear path which is right. I stormed up through the bushes, delighting in going the "wrong" way.

The rest of the camping trip was much more fun. I baked a chocolate cake for breakfast, nesting my small pot of batter into the large pot with three pebbles and a little water in the bottom. I didn't move my campsite *once.* I watched the beavers in the lake, read a book, swam, and ate all of one day. I looked at the map and chose places to explore on day hikes and then changed my mind as I went along. I didn't have to figure out which was the right way, and after that one charge up through the scratchy bushes, I realized I didn't have to go the wrong way either. In fact, there weren't right and wrong ways. There were just lots of choices.

11. Paul

During the years when I worked for the Indian scientists, I travelled to Indian schools all over the country to help teachers become more comfortable about teaching science. Because the United States government had decided early on that Indian children didn't need to learn certain things, there was no tradition of science instruction in most Indian schools. And because many of the teachers I worked with were graduates themselves of these schools, they had never had any formal science education and thought they didn't know anything about science. Of course, every American tribal group has centuries of scientific tradition behind it. It's just not labelled "science." The exquisitely engineered tipi, ancient astronomical observatories, the wonder of Hopi dry farming, the birch-bark canoe, as well as thousands of other technological, agricultural, and medical feats, attest to the long, rich history of science and engineering among American Indians. But these achievements were never thought of as science, something separate from religion, economics, social structure, and so on.

A gratifying part of my job was watching people begin to recognize their own scientific knowledge in their tribes' traditions. Another satisfaction for me was to learn about these things from them and to be among people who felt as I did that the lines drawn between academic disciplines are, after all, arbitrary and certainly shouldn't prevent one from sloshing elements of all of them together. Or, no, it isn't really a matter of mixing things, but simply of not insisting on separating things which are facets of a whole.

There had been a lot of friction between the elders of the tribe and the staff of Four Winds School at Devil's Lake, North Dakota. So, when the tribe took over administration of the school from the Bureau of Indian Affairs, the first thing the new principal did was to hire all the elders, and not to do some useless make-work but to do what they would have done in the past, be elders. The idea intrigued me and I was eager to visit the school and do the one-day workshop they had requested.

When the staff came into the cafeteria where I had set up the equipment for them to experiment with, I tensed. Although I thought hiring the elders had been a wise thing for the principal to do, I was afraid they would resent my being there. This was what I had been dreading ever since starting this job, being confronted by some angry tribal leaders who saw me as part of the white establishment trying to subjugate their people. The fact that I worked for an Indian organization had made me acceptable everywhere I had gone so far, but I was afraid my white skin was going to get me in trouble sooner or later.

After brief introductions, the large group split into clumps of two or three people and started visiting the piles of household objects I had set on tables throughout the room. I'd taped a different page of questions on each table to start them off. They watched pill bugs in a box of dirt and leaf litter. They invented things with a pile of D batteries, some copper wire, and flashlight bulbs. They taped their thumbs to their hands and tried to tie a shoe, fasten a button, and write their names. They played with cornstarch and water, watched dried corn sink and rise in a glass of Sprite, used water droplets as magnifying lenses, lay on a bed of nails and tried to figure out why it didn't hurt, and made kaleidoscopes from plexiglass and duct tape.

Shortly after a group had called me over to where they were fiddling with some dowsing rods, it happened. I saw him walking slowly, deliberately toward me from across the large cafeteria. His braided hair rested on either side of his chest. I tried to prepare myself for the assault, knowing, however, that it was too late.

Then, stepping right through the barriers that should have separated us—differences of age, sex, race, education, language, religious background—he said to me, "I see the rods do the same thing in your hands that they do in mine." My armor clattered to the floor all around me. This was no attack, but a recognition of kinship. I was too startled to speak. "Can you do other things?" he asked.

I wasn't sure what he meant, but I said, "No, I don't think so."

"I think you can."

I had nothing to say but stood disarmed, thinking about that. "Can you put your hands in boiling water?" he asked.

Whatever happened to Hello, I'm so-and-so; nice to meet you? The freedom from these formalities washed around me, making me feel light and relaxed. But boiling water? "No... not without getting burned," I answered. Then, recognizing the implication, I asked, "Can you?"

"Yes. Ever since I was a child."

"Are your hands... different from other people's?"

"No." He extended his hands toward me, palms up, in an invitation for me to touch them and see for myself that they were the same as mine. The demonstration, however, was a failure because as my fingertips brushed his palm, something like an electric shock pulsed through my arm and I jerked it away.

"You notice things in the world and try to figure them out," he said with a smile. "That's what I do. You also enjoy the things you can't figure out." That, in fact, was only a recently acquired skill, and still developing. It felt good to have it appreciated.

The old man spoke briefly about curiosity, awe, explanation, and reverence, noting that neither of us seemed to see a dichotomy between things practical and things spiritual. He ended by saying that he and I both wanted the same thing for the children of his tribe, a chance to explore, play, wonder and love.

I was not surprised when a middle-aged woman approached me a few minutes later and said, "That was Paul. He's our medicine man."

12. Grizzly

One Saturday during a several-week trip to schools on five reservations in Montana, I drove to a trailhead in Glacier National Park so I could spend the day hiking. At the last minute, I put on my Bear Claw earrings, even though I don't usually wear earrings when I'm hiking.

A couple hours down the trail, I heard a rush of wind in the cliff above me and then a gunshot. I was confused; no one should be shooting in a national park. Looking up the steep slope beside me, I saw a rock slide headed straight for me.

That sound hadn't been a gun. It was a rock exploding as it smashed on a ledge from a great height. I ran as fast as I could. When I looked back I saw the slide fanning out to the sides, getting broader as it progressed, so I ran some more. By then it was roaring as if to announce the end of the world. I kept running, and the rock slide thundered down the mountain, covering the part of the trail where I had been a minute before. I stood and looked at that pile of rocks for a long time. Until the roar in my head and the dust in the air settled somewhat.

Then I walked on. The trail skirted below a large granite outcrop. On the far side of it, I stopped short and looked at the grizzly bear standing a few meters above me to my right. His eyes were moist. I couldn't stop looking at them. His legs stiffened and he threw his head from side to side. Then he leapt into the air right toward me.

My legs made the decision to run without consulting my head which knew that the cardinal rule of dealing with grizzlies is NEVER RUN.

I was about to die. I knew that. There was no question. It would be a second or maybe two and the huge paw would bat me down as if I were a mouse. But my legs did not stop straining for speed as if it were important. Did ten seconds pass or ten minutes? I realized I wasn't dead. That paw was overdue. After a bit, my curiosity became intense. I had to look back even though turning would slow me down. I was going to die anyway, so what difference did it make? I took a quick glance backward and studied the after-image in my brain. There were some scrawny little trees, a talus slope, a lot of blue sky. But no bear. I turned again. No, there was definitely no bear behind me. I stopped running and looked randomly about. Far below me, 'way down the mountain, was a bear still moving downhill.

I hiked the rest of the day, singing at the top of my lungs, running from time to time. I had so much energy that I had to jump up and down sometimes. And I couldn't keep from grinning, not that I actually tried.

Driving back to the cabin I'd rented, I passed Sacred Dancing Waters and wondered if it was

Sacred
Dancing Waters
(a place where sacred waters dance)
or
Sacred Dancing
Waters
(waters by which people did sacred dance).

I flew back to Colorado in a few days. Just as the plane's wheels were about to touch the runway, we suddenly tilted wildly to the right. Then we went straight up in the air, or as straight as a plane can go. I felt a huge, soft club hitting me over the head and a cosmic voice said, "You will come to terms with your mortality!" Laughing, I promised I would. The plane landed safely on a second attempt.

13. Neighbors

Ellie and I stopped in Farmington, New Mexico, for gas. A blond teenager filled our tank and chatted amiably with us. "Where are you headed?"

"Shiprock."

Alarm replaced his smile with a stiff, frightened mask. "Oh. You don't want to go there," he warned in a tight, low voice. "That's on the Navajo Reservation and it's gonna be full of Indians today. They're having a big Indian thing there. A big fair or something."

"Yeh," explained Ellie brightly, "that's why we're going there. We're going to the Yeibichai·" The boy stared at us, uncertain what to do or say. Apparently concluding that we must simply be ignorant, he decided to educate us about the danger we were courting.

"I don't think you understand," he began. "There won't be any white people there. It's all Indians. I don't think you wanta be there, especially today." Seeing our enthusiasm undampened, he tried to impress upon us the gravity of the situation. "People get *killed* there!" he nearly shouted.

Struck by the boy's obvious terror of his neighbors and his earnest attempt to protect his white sisters, we, nevertheless, headed on toward Shiprock, undaunted. Within minutes, we found ourselves a part of a monumental desert traffic jam. Old pick-up trucks surrounded us. We all sat for periods of 10, 15, even 20 minutes at a time, then crept forward a few meters. This procedure placed us in prolonged proximity to the occupants of the pick-up cabs on either side of us. Open windows created the illusion that the eight or ten of us were sitting together on a bench. We were all snacking, and after a while, it seemed natural to acknowledge our closeness by sharing our food with each other. Wheat Thins passed from us to the shy little boy to our left. Piñon nuts came back from his mother. Digestive biscuits went out our other window and were answered by fry bread. We inched forward as a unit until the movements of our three lanes gradually de-synchronized and we acquired new neighbors.

Remarkably, no one seemed the least irritated by the long, tedious creep into Shiprock. I began to realize that the party had already begun. People weren't waiting to celebrate until they reached the town. The fair was taking place now in all the truck cabs pointing toward Shiprock. A gay, festive atmosphere suffused the dusty traffic jam. People called to one another and passed food from window to window. True, we couldn't understand the words because everyone else was speaking Navajo, and people were more guarded with us than with the others. Our Farmington informant had been right about one thing: we were the only white people around. But we were a part of the gathering, even if not a full part.

After finally parking our little Toyota in the dirt among the sage and trucks, we walked around the fairgrounds for several hours, taking in the rodeo events (calf roping and bull riding), the dance competition, the crafts and cooking exhibits. Children demonstrated to small audiences of appreciative parents how to saddle a horse, weave a basket, make fry bread, or care for a sheep. Livestock were judged. People sampled jams and looked at exhibits about health care, school construction, and youth clubs. It felt like a cross between a county fair and a Rendezvous from the last century. In one building I was startled to see a videotape of a teacher who had attended one of my workshops. He was standing in the desert delivering a message in Navajo. I don't know what he was talking about, but it felt good to see him looking so confident and poised on the TV screen.

As night fell, the powwow began. People of all ages, dressed in beautiful costumes, danced to the compelling music of five huge drums, each drum surrounded by a circle of singers who also beat the drum. If you stand near one of the enormous drums, the sound resonates in your chest, making you feel you're part of the instrument. The colorful costumes shook and flowed with the movement of the dancing.

Around 11 p.m., Ellie and I began looking for the Yeibichai, the healing ceremony that we had come to attend, having been told about it by the Navajo janitor at Chaco Canyon Visitors' Center. Searching the fairgrounds, we found nothing that looked like a ceremony. We asked a couple people who didn't know or chose not to speak English. We began to wonder if perhaps we were not welcome. At last a young woman responded to our question by looking out of the fairgrounds and saying that the ceremony was by a hogan over there. It still took us another hour, wandering around blinded by the grit-laden wind, to find the spot.

Hundreds of brown faces reflected the light from a large circle of piñon fires. The distinctive desert fragrance from the flames reached out with the light. The warmth, however, didn't stretch as far into the cold night. Ellie and I stood shivering at the outer edge of the circle.

After a few minutes, a group of men painted white and carrying rattles and evergreen sprigs walked into the center of the circle before the hogan. They faced each other in two short lines and began chanting and dancing as they shook their rattles. I couldn't follow the pattern of either music or movement. I wondered how they could. And looking out from my down jacket and wool hat, I wondered why these virtually naked men were not stiff with cold. But stiff they were not as they danced round and round in the ritual movement of the Yeibichai. When they finished, they filed away through the crowd to a brush arbor.

Shortly after the dancers left, an older man standing nearby turned and informed us, "They started dancing at midnight. They'll come back and dance until..." He had trouble describing in English the time of the ending of the ceremony. It had something to do with fading stars or perhaps with the appearance of a particular star and was, I guessed, just before dawn.

A few minutes later, when the dancers returned—or was it a different group that time?—our neighbor told us softly to watch the coyote, the man with the furry tail attached to his waist. Meanwhile, the patient had been ushered out of the hogan. He sat in an aluminum and nylon-webbing lawn chair before the door and at the head of the double line of dancers.

He sat, our neighbor explained, because he was very old and sick. Ordinarily, the patient would stand. This time, as the dance flowed toward the hogan and then curled back in two lines, the coyote man playfully bonked the patient's head with his... Were they juniper branches?... and called out what were apparently humorous taunts to help frighten away the sickness in the old man. By the end of this cycle, I was beginning to feel the rhythm of the chant and to feel the repetition of both music and movement.

As the cold desert night swung toward morning, we succumbed completely to the hypnotic effect of the perfumed air, the glowing, golden faces around the fire circle, and the constant repetition by many groups of dancers of the same few-minute sequence. The chant continued in our minds even during the long periods when the dancers returned to the brush arbor.

It may have been about 3 a.m. when our self-appointed interpreter asked us at a break in the dancing where we were going to sleep after the ceremony. I knew we had set up our tent amidst the sage somewhere before we reached Farmington, but just then in the golden wash of Yeibichai I couldn't place that patch of desert in my mental map. In fact, the map had all but disintegrated. I looked stupidly at our friend and finally said, "Somewhere near Farmington." For the second time in less than a day, I saw a relaxed, friendly face freeze in fear.

"Farmington?" he barely whispered. "You can't sleep there." Seeing that we were ignorant of the danger we were in, he added urgently, "You don't understand. People get *killed* there."

Wow. What clutched fear there was in these two communities on either side of the Navajo Reservation border. And not without cause, I imagined. People probably do get killed both in Farmington and in Shiprock. The more frightened people are, the more violence is apt to erupt. And the more injury that occurs, the more intense the fear. Famous pairs of warring neighbors flitted through my mind: Appalachia's Hatfields and McCoys, Northern Ireland's Protestants and Catholics, India and Pakistan. And yet somehow, we two ingenuous strangers were warmly welcomed in both these frightened towns. Welcomed and assimilated to the extent that each community wanted to protect us from the other. Convection currents of affection and sadness swirled and eddied inside my core. We thanked our guardian and said we would be sure to find a safe place to camp, not mentioning that it seemed we, as outsiders, were safe in either of these worlds.

Still later, our friend asked, "Do you think the old man will get well?"

I thought about it and said, "I think he'll be healed by the ceremony. When it's over, he'll be ready to live or to die." For some reason, that thought made me aware of a hollowness in the center of my chest, a hollowness surrounding a dense, armored nut. I was not ready to die.

14. Michael WhirlwindSoldier

My work at the school in Pierre, South Dakota, was finished. I stopped by the office to say good-bye to the assistant principal, who obviously ran the school. The principal was actually a used-car salesman who had been hired a few weeks earlier. No experience with education, administration, or children. But he was a man and white, so, according to the Bureau of Indian Affairs, better qualified for the job than the Pueblo woman who had served the school for many years as assistant principal.

She asked me what my plans were for the rest of the day. The only thing on my agenda was driving to the Rosebud

Reservation to conduct a workshop the next day. So, when she asked if I would like to teach a science class, I said yes. She was a smart administrator and knew how to take advantage of the few resources that found their way to this under-staffed, under-equipped school for Indian children in trouble with the law. Then she told me that I would be with the special ed group—I could only imagine who in this population of troubled children would be picked out as needing "special education"—and that the two hour class would start in 15 minutes. Oh.

I followed her directions down into the cellar, under the arms of the octopus furnace, and to a locked door. I was certain I must have taken a wrong turn, but a young woman holding a paperback mystery in her hand opened the door when I knocked and led me through the bare room to another door, which she opened for me, locking it again behind me.

I stood startled for a moment, for there in the concrete room—a room protected by two locked doors—under a high, barred window stood a boy, perhaps 11 or 12. I had been told that the class was presently in the shop for their carpentry lesson and that I would have a few minutes alone to set up. I introduced myself. The boy told me he was Michael WhirlwindSoldier. I asked if he would like to be my lab assistant—it seemed the thing to do—and he said he thought he would.

He was fascinated by the objects I pulled from my suitcase and quickly recognized the potential of certain combinations. Soon he was burning steel wool and causing light bulbs to shine, always with a shy look for permission before conducting each experiment. He astounded me by figuring things out in seconds which often stumped rooms full of adults for days at a time.

Then the rest of the class exploded into the room like a bursting seed pod. For the following two hours, Michael and I led the other boys through a series of investigations involving water, fire, electricity, scissors, forks, nails, and other ordinary objects and phenomena. Michael, after an initial impulse to show the others all that he could do with the equipment, proved quite skillful at helping them experience a sense of discovery for themselves. I was impressed.

When we brought out the dowsing rods, two boys lunged at them at once and fell into a wrestling match to determine who would use them first. During the struggle, they toppled a bookcase on a boy who lay sprawled in an apparently drugged sleep on the floor. We all took a few minutes to re-erect the shelf and set the books back in it. The boy on the floor never moved and the teacher seemed unsurprised, making me wonder what sort of drug he had been given and by whom. The class time continued along its bumpy course. At its end, I packed up my things and wandered up to the teachers' lounge to say good-bye.

"No one knows how he got out," a large man in an orange plastic chair was saying as I walked in. "He was cuffed to the bed frame, of course. And the windows in the dorm are barred. Anyway, he went into town and set a bar on fire."

"Oh, that's nothing compared to the time he stabbed that grocer with his own knife," offered another teacher through the aromatic mist rising from his coffee mug. "That kid's outa control."

"I heard Michael WhirlwindSoldier once killed a kid here at school. Is that true?" asked a young man trying vainly to disguise his fear as curiosity.

"Naw, I don't think so," reassured the authoritative voice from the orange chair. "He mighta started that story himself, you know, to scare the other kids, make him look like a big man. Of course, that doesn't mean he won't *hurt* the other kids every time he gets a chance. Knives, burning cigarettes, ropes, you name it. And he used to bite the staff. Doesn't do that anymore. I don't know why. But you remember that tall, skinny fella? What was his name? Taught history, I think. Didn't last too long here. His hand got infected bad from one of WhirlwindSoldier's bites. In fact, maybe that's when he left."

I was, of course, shocked to my core. These people were sitting around swapping Michael WhirlwindSoldier stories in an almost competitive way. These stories of violence and sadism were about the intelligent little boy with whom I had just spent the afternoon.

I thought about him all the way to Rosebud. Expectations. Of course, that's important. I didn't know about Michael's past, so I asked him to be my lab assistant. (Images of the scissors, matches, forks, and so on, swept through my mind.) Given how he's usually treated by adults, he must have been surprised and flattered. But this wasn't wisdom on my part, just lucky ignorance. Lucky for Michael and for me.

And I'm not so naive as to think that we could have rolled along indefinitely in our cozy relationship. Of course, he'd have had to test my affection and respect. In fact, I mused, it may have been a part of our luck that we had only an afternoon together. In this way, Michael is left with a pure memory of having been treated as an intelligent, likable human being. That impression would, no doubt, have been muddied by further involvement with me. Of course, having an on-going relationship with a caring adult would be wonderful for this little boy; but since I wasn't available for that, perhaps it's good that we had time only for the honeymoon and not for the disillusionment.

It was not my habit to read up on the reservations I was going to visit. I don't know if this was more from laziness or a desire to arrive without preconceptions. At any rate, the exception to this rule was my first visit to the Rosebud

Reservation in South Dakota the day after meeting Michael WhirlwindSoldier. By chance, I had read a series of articles about the horrendous conditions on that reservation. They were full of stories of corruption, poverty, abuse. Quack doctors performing fatal surgery. Rape victims avoiding police for fear of being arrested on some charge the rapist made. Children freezing to death in cars. And so on. As I drove through the stark, dusty reservation, past squalid frame houses, I could believe what I had read.

St Francis School was bigger than I had imagined. I stood in the dirt parking lot a couple minutes just taking in the hundred-year-old building, the mobile homes which served as staff housing, the bleak landscape. Odd, but on the drive there I had been thinking about the grand, expansive landscape, cut into fantastic badlands at some places. Now it struck me as bleak.

With that thought, I stepped into the dark building. But I stopped again, involuntarily, just inside the door. Something was wrong. Something was off. There was a dissonance between what was in my head and what I sensed in the school. I stood several minutes, unable to put my finger on the incongruity. Then I knew.

Children's laughter. The articles hadn't mentioned anything about that. Of course not. They were about what was wrong at Rosebud. But of course, children laugh. And, I supposed, adults do too, on occasion. And they probably do all sorts of other natural, ordinary and extraordinary things.

After locating my contact person, Chris Bordeaux, I took a few minutes to fulfill a promise. Michael WhirlwindSoldier, on learning that I was heading for St Francis, had asked me to carry his greetings to his sister.

15. Magic Children

I returned to St Francis for the school science fair the

following spring. The awards ceremony over—everyone got a medal - the chairs and hamsters and tipis and bean plants and windmills were quickly pushed aside. In the middle of the room, a group of men started beating an enormous drum and singing. Chris appeared beside me and explained that the local drum (the musicians) had written an honoring song for all the children at the school, just as they would to celebrate an achievement by any community member. Young women holding babies, men in cowboy boots, the St Francis students and their older siblings, stooped old women and stiff old men began to flow around the drum. The dancing circle grew until it filled the room, leaving no one outside it. I wiped my eyes with my coat sleeve—we were all wearing coats in the unheated gym on that March evening on the northern plains—and joined the dance.

Throughout that spring and in subsequent springs, I had the thrill of seeing such miracles take place all over Indian Country. Each community grew a science fair from its own roots, following no rules but its own, supporting and supported by tribal traditions.

At the Quileute Tribal School, a converted Coast Guard station dangling off the northwest corner of the country, a boy and a girl, both about nine years old, told me excitedly how they had decided on the subject of their project. They had noticed that the water coming from the taps on the reservation had a rusty color, unlike water in Forks, a town a few miles inland. So, they set up an experiment. They washed dirty rags in each type of water, cold and hot, with and without detergent and with and without bleach. The results of their complex experiment were hung up like a janitor's laundry. Their conclusion: the harder you try to clean things with Quileute water, the dirtier they get. This conclusion sounded familiar to me, like something I had learned long ago. And the dirty rags. They reminded me of something, too, something disquieting. But I couldn't remember what.

At Red Cloud School on the Pine Ridge Reservation in South Dakota, I learned from a sixteen-year-old girl about a traditional Lakota healing ceremony. When I asked the girl how she had chosen this subject to study, she said that she was alive now only because a medicine person had cured her of a severe illness as a child. She remembered the experience of "coming back alive" and wanted to learn more about how the healing had been done. Unaccountably, I envied this ragged, illiterate girl.

In Oregon I met a boy who had never shown any interest in studies until he'd been sent to an alternative school for kids who were in trouble. In previous years, he'd spent most of his time skipping school and shooting guns. But with the support of his new teacher, John produced a project that won him international honors. The reason he was at the reform school was that he had gotten too far behind in his studies when he was shot in the face and had to spend several months in the hospital. His mother told me through tightly held lips that a year ago she could have imagined attending a funeral or a trial, but not an international awards ceremony. Opportunity sometimes comes dressed as tragedy.

While John and a Blackfeet girl marched down the aisle at the opening ceremony of the International Science and Engineering Fair, dressed in tribal finery, carrying an eagle staff, and moving to the strong, piercing voices of Howard BadHand and his cousin, I asked the girl's teacher if he had gotten some good pictures. He fumbled with his camera, partially covered his face with one hand, and replied, "I don't know. I can't see too well right now."

At Acoma Pueblo in New Mexico, still weak from the salmonella which had kept me vomiting much of the previous night, I took frequent rests from judging the science fair. Fortunately, an English friend, Gwen Hampshire, had joined me on this trip. So, she filled in for me in most of my duties. The children weren't sure where England was, but they knew it wasn't nearby. They were impressed that someone had come so far to talk to them.

It was while taking a break during that fair that the reality of fetal alcohol syndrome finally lined up in my head with what I had read about it. Those scrawny children surrounding the special-ed planetarium—they were fetal alcohol kids.

Of course.

And there were other, less extreme examples among their classmates. Sunken nasal bridge, thin upper lip, oddly shaped eyes.

Suddenly the room was full of these features. I thought back to the other schools I'd visited and the inordinately large proportion of disabled children at them. This was it. I had been hearing about it and seeing it everywhere, but I was only now taking it in. This was a crisis. A generation of disabled children. And part of their syndrome is an inability to understand cause and effect. They are also born addicted to alcohol. These children would have children and they would drink through their pregnancies—because they are alcoholic and because they don't understand that it will harm their babies—and their children will be born with the same syndrome. I slipped into a quiet despair at the edge of the colorful, happily noisy cafeteria.

Suddenly I became aware of a young voice close at hand.

"Excuse me?", I said

"Do you want to see my project?" the small girl repeated. "It's about piñon trees. I love piñon trees."

The St Francis effect again. All is not lost if a child laughs or loves piñon trees.

16. Haunted Hotel

Although I didn't usually use an alarm to wake myself, I

decided to set one just in case. I'd just flown back from the Pacific time zone and, despite my neurotic protection of sleep times, was operating on a severe sleep deficit, so 7 a.m. was going to arrive before I expected it. Yes, an alarm would be a good idea. After a few false attempts, I figured out the hotel-room clock radio, turned off the dazzling overhead—why on earth did they have such bright lights?—and crawled under the tasteful bedcover (of the same fabric as the tasteful curtains and in colors to complement the tasteful carpeting and upholstery). Such sumptuous accommodations felt unjustifiably extravagant after years of simple, sometimes rough housing on Indian reservations.

Completely discombobulated, I squinted my already closed eyes, noted the unfamiliar smell of the pillow under my right cheek, and began slowly to realize that I must have been asleep, that I was not at home, that I was not alone. I remained purposely still and blind long after full alertness had set in. Why give away that I was awake?

I knew I was to have a roommate during the conference, but she wasn't due to arrive for another day. But this must be—what was her name? I listened through resentment to the sounds of her unpacking and getting ready for bed. It would be over soon. I wouldn't say anything. But the shower clanged on and on and the overhead blazed. Surreptitiously I dragged a corner of bedcover over my eyes. Gads, that was strong perfume or deodorant or whatever whooshing out with the thwanging bathroom door.

At last the rustling and rattling faded.

A strong alto voice suddenly boomed, "Hi! It's Susan. Yeh. I'm in Denver... Well, no, everything *didn't* go OK, but, anyway, I got here..."

That phone call must have lasted 30 minutes. The second was at least as long and twice as animated. When I heard the third commence, I could hardly keep from shrieking. Eventually, though, the bellowing ceased and I could practically taste the sleep overtaking my weary mind and body.

The flavor had not fully matured, though, before a machine gun wrenched me back into full, if furious wakefulness. What on earth? The sound originated only a meter from my ear. I risked a slitted eye and peaked out from under the covers. Susan—that's right, that was her name—sat on the next bed cutting heavy poster board with an industrial strength pair of shears. The large empty suitcase the operation rested on served as a laudable sound box. I knew it was empty even before I had experienced its amplifying qualities. I had heard each item placed in the rattling, scraping dresser drawers or hung on the clanging coat hangers in the closet with the squeaky door and the thudding latch.

Soon, a crunching joined the machine gun shears and was accompanied shortly by the strong fragrance of chocolate mint. I knew those cookies and usually liked them. But now my body revolted against the pull into such daytime tasks as salivation. It wanted only to be unconscious, to rest. The smell and sound of food was nauseating.

Fatigue made every part of me heavy. Leaden tears dragged out of my left eye, rolled across the bridge of my nose, joined others from my right eye and wicked into the funny-smelling pillow slip. Its scent was a sickening mixture of disinfectant and old tobacco smoke. You'd think that a high-class hotel...

I startled awake. My automatic, completely dependable, utterly trustworthy, maddeningly consistent, infuriatingly out-of-control wake-up mechanism had detonated. I never missed meetings, appointments, planes, busses. But I sometimes missed a lot of sleep the night before an important rendezvous, waking every fifteen or thirty minutes. It was dark. What time was it? Where was I? The clock radio. Right. Over here. My hand fumbled against the bedside table and the appliance. I pressed all over the clock, trying to find the face. At last I turned it so the digital read-out was visible to my head on the strange pillow. 4:23. Well, I've got a couple more hours to sleep. Come on, Kit, just relax. No need to do this bouncing awake thing. Take it easy. Turn the clock around so your roommate can see it if she needs to.

Panicking, I lurch awake again, fumble over the radio's surface. 4:56. Go back to sleep.

5:14. 5:32. Gees. Sleep!

At 6:36, I capitulated, as I always do surrender after a night like that. In the shower, I fought the usual nausea by hoping the noise irritated Susan as much as it had me.

I had noticed a 24-hour grocery store in the neighborhood the previous day and had planned to go there for some breakfast food before convening the meeting at 8. At least this part of my plan worked, even if the get-to-bed-early-and-rest-up-for-the-big-event part had failed.

My rice cakes and soy milk finished—my escalating food allergies made ordinary breakfasts out of the question—I made my way to the conference room and re-checked the piles of information, charts, questionnaires, and supplies I had set out the previous evening at each person's place at the large oval table. Nothing missing. Nothing out of order. Of course.

It was still early. I picked up my coat and headed for first floor. I took a walk around the shops and restaurants and lounges of the hotel's ground floor. Interior decoration. That seemed to be the style. Not Victorian or frontier or space-age. "Interior decoration". Tasteful ensembles of furniture. Muted colors. It wasn't any style at all. Just inoffensive. But not even that, really. It was all so big, so expensive, so artificial, so disconnected from the planet it was on. I hurtled out the double double doors (2 sets, you know) into the equally surreal outdoor environment. I tried to walk around the hotel but got cut off where the artificial-feeling lawn ended abruptly at the top of a high concrete wall. Traffic streamed through the noxious air below me. I scanned the area for something natural, some reminder of our animality, some connection to the cycling of nutrients through the environment, some acknowledgement of the flow of energy from sun to green plants to us. The prickly grass didn't do it for me. I couldn't really believe it was photosynthetic. The noisy lace of highways was no help. I retreated back to the unreality of the hotel done in interior-decoration style.

It must be time for me to convene the education committee meeting anyway. I took the elevator to the third floor. No one in the conference room yet. That's weird. Maybe I should buy a watch sometime. Better check the clock in my room. Elevator to 15th floor. Susan's still asleep. Actually, hardly anyone is up, come to think of it. The place is nearly deserted. 7:51, the clock radio tells me. Elevator back to third. They'll all be there now. But, no, not a soul. I sit in a chair at the middle of one long side of the table. I'd already rejected the traditional head seat. Can't see people well or hear them or speak to them. Didn't like the symbolism anyway. Right in the thick of it. That's where I wanted to be in this committee meeting, not at the top but in the middle. Actually, not in the thick of things, I realized on second thought, but to be out of the spot light, just one of the folks. I didn't want prominence but anonymity, even invisibility.

Still no one here. This is genuinely weird. I pace, stand in the hallway, walk over to the elevators, come back.

When I was sure that it must be after 8:30, half an hour late for the meeting, I took the elevator to first floor and asked the time at reception. "Seven twenty-five."

"Excuse me?"

"Seven twenty-five. Actually seven twenty-three."

I returned to the elevator bay slightly dazed. What was going on? Third floor conference room. What was I doing there? No one would be here for... What time was the meeting? Eight. And the guy at the desk said it was half past seven. Well, they will start coming in 15 minutes or so, I guessed.

What was this with the weird time? The clock radio! The buttons I pushed accidentally in the dark or the trouble I had setting the alarm. That must be it. I must have reset the time. So, I think it's an hour later than it is. Maybe I'll go lie down in my room for a few minutes. 15th floor.

"Hi! You must be Kit. You were sure zonked out last night when I arrived. Hope I didn't bother you."

Quick greetings, feigned hurry, and I was back down at the conference room.

The meeting had barely begun when a boy arrived with an urgent phone message. Yes, he was sure I needed to call back immediately. Apologies. Instructions. A promise to return quickly. And down to the hurricane-struck conference headquarters.

At first I didn't even realize that the phone wasn't working, the noise in my other ear was so great. No, no one else knew how to work the phone or even if it did work. Better ask at the front desk. A man eventually freed himself from the expanding crowd at the desk and came back to the office with me. Tinker, plug, unplug, plug. "Did you dial 9-2 for an outside line?.. .Well, that's it: 9-2."

Sure enough, the call went through. One frantic office to another. "Kit, this is an emergency..." The urgent voice gave me detailed directions for finding a piece of paper in a folder in a box in the disaster area of the conference office. But the box, when I finally located it, was actually not in the office but in a room down the hall. This all took a lot of time. I was pretty anxious about the committee meeting that had barely begun before I left. What's more, as I noted the instructions about locating the important Paper, the ballpoint I borrowed leaked viscous blue ink all over my right hand. I'd meticulously avoided using it throughout the paper search—a bit of a nuisance—but something had to be done about it before I returned to my meeting. What would they be doing by now, abandoned by their chairwoman for... How long had I been gone? A watch would be a good idea.

But first, a ladies' room. Why do they hide them? Here's one at the end of this dark hall. Under the pressure of my thumb, the little lever labeled PUSH at first resisted, then moved sharply an inch closer to the wall over the sink. Liquid soap splattered all over my chest. I flinched at the droplets hitting my face. Inspecting the damage, I realized my socks and shoes were the only unaffected garments. Later. I'd deal with that later. First the Rorschach Test on my hand. In fact, I was able only to smear and lighten the dark ink, giving my right hand a ghastly grey pall. It would have to do. A committee was waiting for me to lead them.

The foam produced by a quick rub with a wet paper towel on my skirt made it instantly clear that the outfit was not salvageable for use today. I'd have to change clothes. Elevator up to 15th. But the hotel was getting crowded now with the hundreds of conference attenders. I had to wait for the third car before there was room for me, and we stopped for comings and goings on nearly every floor.

At least Susan was gone when I got to the room. No time wasted on embarrassing explanation. Clothes off. Quick sudsy shower. The nausea and dizziness were exacerbated this time by the disconcerting feeling that I was becoming a cartoon, exuding bubbles with each movement. Fresh slip, underpants, skirt and blouse. Glance in the mirror. No unzipped zippers, mismatched buttons and buttonholes.

Nothing obvious, *except* my blue-grey corpse hand. It would have to do.

I stood with a rotund little man before the elevators. After what seemed like a long time, a door opened and the little man started to step in the car, but suddenly the doors began to shut on his extended leg. He leapt back into the hallway and we both watched as the doors did a horror-film dance, crashing shut, opening half way, shutting again, opening for a tantalizingly long time—should we get on?—then lurching half-way closed and open again. There was no regularity to the movement. It did not elicit our confidence. A second elevator arrived, but it was too crowded to admit even one more passenger. In frustration, I jumped on the haunted elevator—the little man declined to join me—and pressed the CLOSE DOOR button. The doors closed. I wasn't sure if that was good or bad. I pressed 3rd and waited. The machine seemed to get the hiccups. I wished I hadn't gotten on. Gees, I would be trapped in here for the rest of the day and never get back to my committee. What time was it, anyway? Why didn't I look at the clock radio in the room? Of course I hadn't taken time to do that, I'd been in such a hurry. Maybe I would buy a watch when I got back home. Did I say trapped? I lunged at the OPEN DOOR button. Nothing happened. Then the doors jerked half-way open and I leapt into the hallway.

The gnome was gone. I guess the other elevator had come again. Or else he gave up and took the stairs. Stairs! There must be stairs. There'd have to be for fire safety. I scoured the halls and finally located a door marked FIRE EXIT. Good idea to know where this was anyway. I checked it to see if it was the type which set off an alarm when it was opened. Explanations to the fire brigade would just be too much for one morning. Seemed OK.

I hurtled down the grey concrete stairs, flight after flight, until I was quite dizzy from the tight turns. There was the door labeled 5th. Almost there. 3rd. I threw my weight extra vigorously at the heavy fire door, partly from the momentum of my descent, partly from the excitement of finally being done with this comic interlude. In fact, now that it was over, the morning struck me as very funny.

The fact that the door didn't open was a shock, both physically because I had crashed so hard against it and emotionally because I wasn't sure I could get out of the stairwell on any floor. And it was *cold* in there. (I'd left my coat in the bedroom.) Unheated. Concrete. Grey. Trapped. I ran down to the door labeled LOBBY. Most likely door to be open. But it wasn't. Systematic. Don't panic. Be thorough. 1st. 2nd. Already tried 3rd. No, try it again, just in case. 4th. This is looking bad. If several doors are locked, why would any be unlocked? I kept seeing a picture of myself shivering on a landing, dying of cold... or would it be thirst? I worked my way up. At least it was getting me warm.

Quite unexpectedly the door on 12th gave way under my hand. Free. Warm. Safe. They won't find me in 1998, a desiccated corpse curled in a corner of the concrete stairwell. I ran elated to the elevator bay and nearly crashed into an old Hopi couple waiting there. How could I explain? I'm not dead! It isn't 1998 and I'm not a skeleton with leathery skin dried on it! No, perhaps a polite smile is better. Miraculously, the elevator car had room for all three of us and was not the one with the hiccups. 3rd.

Outside the conference room door, I stopped and waited for my heart to stop pounding so violently. Fifteen faces turned curiously toward me as I stepped calmly into the room. Some eyes couldn't stop themselves from scanning my transformed attire. Maybe it was more than the clothes, I suddenly thought. My hair must be a mess. The hand. I'd forgotten the blue hand. No one said anything. I looked at the table.

This was a good group. Copies of the agenda were strewn everywhere, names handwritten by several items, underlinings and notes added. Several drafts of letters sat under poised pens. A poster—quite a sophisticated one—was under construction at one end of the table. Two completed ones stood against the far wall. I didn't know what to say. First things first.

"I have to tell you what happened." Several of the expectant faces nodded. We'd never actually all been in the same room before. It was a newly-formed committee, charged with oversight of the organization's educational programs. We were getting big enough to need this sort of support. I knew most of these folks from my travels, and selected others on my colleagues' recommendation. They were good and they clearly knew how to work. And, yes, they deserved an explanation. As the story unfolded, we all got laughing uncontrollably. We sat for a long time wiping our eyes and exchanging one-liners then finished up the work that they had started. What a good group. I felt warm and happy when we broke for lunch.

The next day, I happened to step onto the elevator as one of the committee members got off. He jumped out of the car theatrically, turned and urgently addressed the others pouring into the car. "No, don't get on an elevator with that woman! And don't go into the fire escape with her! And, by all means, don't go into the ladies' room with her!" The doors closed and we rose silently through the shaft. Some people looked assiduously at the closed door or their feet or the ceiling. Others couldn't keep their eyes from flitting in my direction. I popped out on 15th floor and burst into convulsive giggles.

17. Al and Howard

Al Qoyawayma couldn't find a comfortable way to hold his

hands as he stood stiffly in the side gallery of the university museum. But his grey suit, complete with vest, looked as natural on him as Howard BadHand's jeans and soft shirt did on him.

Kneeling on the floor, Howard opened a wooden box from which he drew the sacred objects he would use in the honoring ceremony. A heterogeneous crowd of children and adults, Indians and non-Indians milled around the gallery, most of their attention turned toward Al and Howard in the center of the open room. There was a quiet hum of conversation accompanied by the scuffing of boots, the clicking of dress shoes, and the squeaking of sneakers.

No abrupt break marked the end of the coming together and the beginning of the ceremony. Howard gradually modulated from chatting with Al and the others near him to addressing the entire group as he continued to arrange the eagle feathers, the pipe, the tobacco, the sage, and the other objects he'd taken from his carved box. He reminded us of the purpose of our gathering, the honoring of Al Qoyawayma, Hopi potter and engineer, who had just received an honorary degree from the University of Colorado.

Then, sensing the various levels of ease and disease among those present, Howard encouraged people to do what they needed in order to make themselves comfortable. To make that possible for those whose discomfort arose from their ignorance of what was expected of them at this event, he added, "Sit or stand, whatever feels good to you. If you want to move around, that's fine. You can be quiet if you like, but you don't have to."

He covered the box, set it to the side, and continued slowly in a low voice, "For a time, set aside your worries and your bad feelings and open yourselves to whatever source of peace, energy, creativity, and harmony you recognize. And do whatever seems right when you've opened to that source.

There are no bad choices when you've made that opening." A few people sat down. Others got up. Some children ran behind a room divider and giggled. No one told them to stop.

Howard asked Al to step closer and stand in front of him. Al's hands became even more restless for a moment and then settled into a relaxed hang at his sides. Howard spoke directly to Al. "This ceremony is not to give you the Indian version of an honorary degree. In fact, it is not only for the purpose of honoring you. Since your achievements have, in a sense, separated you from your community, this ceremony is also to bring you back into the group. So, we are here both to honor you, which sets you apart, and to re-form the whole."

I'd been thinking recently about the interaction between individuation and community building. This medicine man, it seemed, didn't see a person's task in life as choosing between these, but as using each to strengthen the other. Al's community supported him as a student and a young man, making it possible for him to excel in his chosen fields. Then he returned to his community, offering the benefits of his talents, now cultivated, strengthened, refined. His community, in turn, supports and honors him, making him better able to continue growing. There was, to me, an appealing rhythm to the process, one which ticked between personal and group development. During the ceremony, Al was neither glorified as better than the rest of us nor castigated for leaving the fold. The event respectfully acknowledged both his personal accomplishments and his group membership.

Howard said a simple prayer, filled the pipe, and invited everyone to smoke. When Al tensed slightly as the pipe was offered him, Howard said quietly and with a smile, "It's OK. I'm not a smoker either." Perhaps because of that reassurance, I decided to join the others participating in that part of the ceremony. Those of us who chose to smoke came into the center of the room and stood in a circle around Howard and

Al. Howard walked around the circle clockwise and handed the pipe to each of us in turn. Some people blew the smoke into their hands and poured it over their heads or washed their faces in it. Suddenly it occurred to me that I'd done this ritual before, the symbolic taking in of a divine energy and the strengthening of a group bond by sharing the experience. But I'd never really felt it as that when I'd knelt at the altar and drunk grape juice and eaten a white wafer.

There was an atmosphere of relaxed reverence in the gallery. People chatted quietly in the group. Others walked about. The casualness did not seem disrespectful. Nor did the solemnity seem rigid or restricting. This was an atmosphere in which anyone could touch the eternal and in which even a stranger could feel at home, more at home than I had ever felt wearing a stiff dress and perched in unnatural stillness on a hard pew in my father's beautiful church.

Or was this comfort a *result* of my being a stranger? Do the sage and the eagle feathers, I wondered, become cloying and confining to someone who grew up with them?

18. The Rain on the Plane

The Lumbee Indians of North Carolina are not recognized by the United States government. They are not officially Indians. What a strange feeling it must be to know you are Indian but also to know you are not. What a surreal state of affairs. Fortunately, official definitions had no bearing on my work. So, when the Lumbees asked me to visit them, I did.

The plane already held about twenty passengers. The only seat left was the one just behind the pilot. As we taxied, hot hills and blue sky streaked by the window. But then, suddenly, it was raining. On me. Inside the plane. Helpless, I looked again at the clear sky for some explanation. As we gained altitude, the shower grew to a downpour. Dizzy and queasy, with a knot in my center, I twisted in my seat belt and looked at the two men across the aisle to my right. One of them cleared his throat and covered his pinched mouth. They both looked away, feigning boredom. Turning completely around, I examined through a sheet of water the dry, amused passengers behind me. The cloudburst was exclusively for me, my private experience.

After a minute or two, the rain stopped. I dabbed at myself with a dry shirt from my carry-on bag. No one laughed aloud or otherwise acknowledged what had happened. Maybe no one had noticed my silly problem. I hoped so. I began to wonder if it really had happened. The flight was long enough that my clothes had dried and I had decided to forget the incident by the time we started our descent.

And then the rain began again. I struggled to lean out of the downpour, but it exactly encompassed the range of my frantic movement. The plane and the rain eventually stopped, and I surveyed the deepened colors of my drenched jumpsuit. I sat a moment, uncertain whether I was about to faint or throw up. I began to shake, my mouth stretched into an involuntary smile, and then the laughter flooded out. As soon as I started, other passengers, relieved now of the burden of pretending not to notice, began to giggle and then to laugh outright. My dizziness and nausea were washed away in the hilarity. Until that moment, I'd been concerned that people might have noticed my predicament. What an enormous relief when I knew that they had, that I hadn't invented the whole thing.

19. Ozzie

"That's my life now, working with kids, so maybe they don't have to do all the stuff I did. Maybe they will anyway, but maybe it won't take 'em so long to get through it." Ozzie had come as the adult sponsor for the kids from Montana. We would all be spending eleven days here in the hills of New Mexico. I had been responsible for recruiting high school students from various reservations around the country. Besides Ozzie's group from Montana, there were four kids from Pine Ridge, South Dakota, and another three from various Pueblos in New Mexico. All these were sponsored by the organization I worked for. The remaining 50 or so came through other channels to this youth leadership camp.

Ozzie had just told me over mac and cheese how he had married as a drunken stunt and realized only years later how demeaning that had been to his wife and to himself. He described how he abandoned his family and lived on the streets, eating garbage and devoting all his energy to keeping drunk. He said he couldn't tell me where he had been all those years; all the cities, all the jails, looked the same. At one point, back with his wife, he yielded to her pleading and checked into an alcohol rehabilitation facility. It was just another stunt as far as he was concerned. He would go play that game, get his wife off his back, and show up the doctors' stupidity. It could be entertaining. But then one day his wife and son came to visit. The small boy turned to his mother as they entered Ozzie's room and asked, "You won't let that mean man come back to our house, will you?"

The question echoed in Ozzie's head. His own son thought of him as "that mean man." Those thin words slid through a tiny chink in Ozzie's armor and pierced his heart. As he explained it to me over our camp lunch, there was no question after that of drinking anymore or living on the street. He threw himself into the program at the treatment center and emerged with a mission to spare others the long, painful detour he had taken away from love and joy.

And so, here he was with a group of teenagers at a camp in the New Mexico mountains. The camp director said that

Ozzie was the most outstanding adult support person ever to accompany a group to one of these events. (A group of kids wanting to attend always has to find a local adult who will join in the program with them and help them implement back home any plans they make while at the camp. Some groups, for example, started telephone hotlines for teenagers. Others persuaded cab companies to give kids free rides home on prom night, to avoid alcohol-related accidents. Others built playgrounds, painted murals, started daycare programs at their schools so teenage mothers didn't have to drop out. And so on.)

On our last evening at the camp, we all met at the campfire circle to listen to a guest speaker. She was a distressingly unbelievable woman who boasted of her magical abilities. I struggled with my judgmentalism and concluded tentatively that she was a hunter who needed more time in the woods. She had made a desperate grasp at the elusive creature of spirituality and had come away with a handful of fur but no meat. In her innocence, she clutched and revered her fluffy catch. I scanned the rest of the audience for confirmation or contradiction of my musing. The incongruity between the speaker's manner and her message was reflected in a half circle of puzzled faces.

The group clapped politely when she finished, and then Ozzie stood before the fire. He was the evening's second speaker. Ninety faces, red with fire light, relaxed under the influence of this man's honest story. Here was real magic. Not dulled by dogma, he glowed with integrity, simplicity.

Without thinking about what I was doing, I stood up from the bench and walked toward Ozzie when he had finished speaking. I reached him just as a half dozen kids got there. And from the corner of my eye, I saw that everyone had risen and was converging in an enormous embrace. The whole camp stood in this hug for several minutes, soaking up the warmth radiating from the orange flames, from Ozzie, and from all of us.

On the last morning of the camp, I awoke feeling disoriented and struggling for breath. Nausea waved through me. In a moment I realized that I was pinned by two or three masked figures while another sprayed me with shaving cream. Completely limp except for a dense knot at my solar plexus, I neither struggled nor screamed; just waited vaguely for them to finish. That seemed a disappointing reaction to them and they eventually left. I heard a scream from another cabin but I still couldn't move.

Eventually, I got up, walked through the pre-dawn to the bathhouse and showered the shaving cream out of my hair and T-shirt. The sickness I'd felt while pinned in my bunk intensified. I worked a while on my sleeping bag, trying to rinse off the foam without soaking the down. I hung it in a tree and then walked aimlessly into the forest.

I walked a long time, aware that I was missing breakfast and good-byes. I kept trying to turn back toward camp but failing. I couldn't face it, them, something. I was completely shaken by the "innocent" attack and could not stop alternately crying and raging.

At last I sat down on the edge of a small ravine. The tears seemed finally to be drained away. The anger was only smoldering now, not flaming. I felt bleak, empty, hopeless. Then I noticed the coyote sitting on the opposite bank of the ravine, some 20 meters away. It sat calmly, returning my gaze. We looked at each other a long time, I don't know, minutes, maybe ten minutes, maybe fifteen. I broke the spell by standing up. The coyote ambled up the ravine. I walked down, toward camp.

I felt calmer, but still rattled. All the kids were gone. So was Ozzie. I wished I had said good-bye. I wished I knew why the incident bothered me so much.

From the perspective of several weeks back at home, I began to see something distressing about the whole program in New Mexico. True, it was efficiently run by good people who sincerely wanted the best for the participants. Every day was full of stimulation, including healthful exercise of several types, reasonably nourishing food, intellectual, moral, social, and physical challenges, work and play in groups of various sizes, and an ever-present undercurrent of the importance of service. All this was true.

So, why was I uncomfortable? It was Georgia who drew the parallel with Hitler Youth. I was shocked. No, certainly I couldn't be involved in something like that. But then, people involved in Hitler Youth events didn't see themselves as reprehensible either. Quite the contrary. They were involved in hygienic, healthful, moral pursuits, exactly as we at the camp would describe ourselves. I looked back at the eleven days. The first clue I picked up that something was amiss was the angry rampage of the last morning (past the danger of any possible punishment). It was definitely anger and not playfulness that sparked the gang of kids who systematically foamed all the staff. They were, I decided, the outlet for the dis-ease present in the group as a whole. The tension resulting from the constant pressure of the program had to be released, the pain expressed. These "bad" kids performed that function for those of us who were too "good" to consider such an act.

What did the pressure consist of? Every minute of every participant's and every staff person's day was scheduled. To make it a rich experience, no doubt, and to waste not a drop of opportunity to uplift, enlighten, and stretch the kids. But underlying that frantic desire to pack as much instruction into the time as possible was fear, a fear that left to themselves, kids will run amok.

Why was there no time for solitude, for silence, for daydreaming, meditation, introspection? These are the other side of the story in most cultures. There is social interaction and there is inner quest. And it is the mix of the two which makes a whole person. So, why did this camp ignore the inner half of these kids' journeys? Because the organizers were terrified by what the students might find inside themselves. This fear was intense because they had never allowed *themselves* to look at their own interiors. Because of their upbringing, they were convinced that they were essentially bad, that we all are, and that strict, energetic training, leaving no time for introspection, was necessary to make moral people of themselves or the children in their care. At least, that was what I imagined to be at the root of the frantic activity.

I was a sucker for this sort of program. It seemed so wholesome, so right, so moral. It was familiar. Nothing blatant, nothing overtly violent. But always the crushing pressure, which none dare label as evil, to be a good person in service of humanity.

Nothing, indeed, is intrinsically wrong with serving humanity, if that service arises from the passionate core of one's being. And that is, in fact, the inevitable result of allowing a person to contact, own, and live from that passionate core. Such a person, respected, supported, and loved for what he or she is rather than for what he or she can be made into, will automatically respect, support, and love others. That person will quite naturally serve humanity because he will be living from his unique core, offering to the world what he loves doing rather than what he has learned he should do. And a gift of love, unlike the dull, heavy gift of duty, illumines and lifts both recipient and giver.

I decided not to work at the following year's youth leadership camp. But another two years would pass before I understood the depth of my reaction to the one I had attended.

20. Before Dinner or After

My friend Sarah had invited me to dinner. We stood in her kitchen telling each other stories of what we'd been up to since we'd last seen each other. Sarah was stirring a pot of some savory sauce. I was impressed, maybe even a bit intimidated, by her cooking skill and ease in the kitchen.

Suddenly I announced, "I want to cut my hair." I had really long hair. It wasn't exactly that I had decided to have long hair. I just never bothered to cut it. I couldn't actually remember when last it had been cut. Years ago, anyway. More than two decades. Let's see. My mother cut my hair when I was little. Then there was the time I was taken to a hair dresser when I was about 9 or 10. What a trauma that was. And that was the last hair cut I could remember. I just never got around to it again after that.

So, in my late thirties, in Sarah's kitchen, I suddenly decided to get a hair cut. Sarah continued stirring the pot and asked casually, "Before dinner or after?"

"Uh. Before." Why wait another minute, in fact? It wasn't as if I had any doubt or hesitation. In the past, when I had thought about the concept of cutting my hair, it was for only a couple seconds. It had been so long since I'd done it that I wasn't sure what it would be like. I'd changed a lot since I was 10. Maybe short hair would look awful on me. That sort of thing. I never seriously considered it. But tonight, it wasn't even a question. It was a certainty. I would get my hair cut. And I didn't care what it looked like. I was suddenly in a hurry to have it gone.

"How do you want it?" Sarah asked, scissors in hand. (She told me later that she'd been waiting for years for me to reach this point and she wasn't going to let me out of her kitchen without a haircut. She needn't have worried. I was not going to change my mind.)

"Off," was all I told her. And that's where it went.

Part IV

BEFORE FORGETTING: LOSING HER WAY
(1949-1952, Toby)

I am falling
I am falling

past star
past time
through space
and my own fragments

From the mythic tradition
of the native women of Vancouver Island
as related by
Anne Cameron in *Daughters of Copper Woman*

There was a little girl. She had blond hair just like her uncle's fantasy little girl. But this girl was real and she knew it, until later she thought maybe that was a mistake. But first she thought she was real.

Her uncle Ned told her secrets and showed her private things that were just for him and her. Her name was Kit. Uncle Ned said he loved her and touched her so softly that his fat finger was like a butterfly made out of meat. Except sometimes he looked scared and his meat butterflies became stiff, heavy clamps that kept her from moving or talking or, sometimes, breathing. His whole body could get heavy like that and crush her. They both got scared then. And sometimes she got stuck with her eyes under that bright light bulb that hung down on a cord from the ceiling, and that hurt her eyes and she couldn't move away.

Maybe Kit died sometimes when she couldn't breathe. I was older and knew some more things and I'm also magic and—my name is Toby—I would come and get Kit and we'd go up through the ceiling like ghosts. So that's why I think maybe she died sometimes. I'm pretty little, like Kit was, but not that little. She was only three. And before that she was so little she didn't know how to talk. I'm much bigger than that. I wear a flour sack with holes for my head and arms. I have black hair that's short and prickly. I never get cold. And I never get scared. And I always tell the truth. And I can make things out of air, like a hammock and a sliding board and a see-saw and other stuff. And Kit and I used to play in the air.

Well, one day Kit turned into a zebra. It was hurt. It's throat was bleeding. And it couldn't get out of bed.

Another day she turned into a coyote and used her sharp teeth to tear the covers off the bad bed. Then she ripped them all up. She always calls the bad bedroom Aunt Minnie's room even though Great Aunt Minnie doesn't come there much. That way she doesn't have to call it its real name, The Bad Bedroom.

Once Kit got really scared and was talking and crying and screaming maybe. That scared Uncle Ned and he held a pillow over her head and told her to be quiet. Of course, that was even scarier for Kit, so she made more noise. So, Uncle Ned had to put the pillow right down over Kit's whole head so he couldn't hear her. A pillow was really good for doing that 'cause it filled in all the spaces around Kit's face so no air could get into her. I'm pretty sure she died that time.

Ned was fat and had dark, greasy hair. He liked his brother-in-law, Bill, who was tall, thin, and handsome. Ned thought maybe they could get talking and Bill might be able to help him figure out about the little blond girl he made up. Ned worried about that little girl who was also Bill's only daughter, the real version, that is. So maybe Bill, who was a good guy and a deep thinker, could help straighten things out.

Bill and Ned loved purple onions. One night at the church camp for ministers they sat under the yellow light bulb on the back porch of Bill's cottage and sliced onion and made sandwiches that were mostly onion. They talked about God and being good and being bad. Ned started talking about bodies and how nice God was to make bodies. Maybe Bill felt attracted to beautiful little girls, too, and it really was all right, Ned was thinking. Maybe they'll start telling the truth the way grown ups can only do late at night and Ned will find out that he isn't any different from his handsome brother-in-law.

But, unfortunately, Bill was very tired and had promised to go into town early in the morning to get sticky buns for breakfast, so he went to bed.

Blood was tickling her leg, but Kit didn't laugh. She never laughed when she was tickled. Well, people thought she laughed, but it was something her body did all by itself that was very scary and happened to sound like laughing.

She ran out of The Bad Bedroom and stood at the top of the stairs and screamed, "Mommy! Mommy!" But no one else was in the cottage.

Then her daddy's voice came shouting from outside, "Kit! Kit!" Her daddy ran into the living room. Kit ran down the stairs very fast saying, "Uncle Ned hurt me! He hurt me!" Only her feet and her words were going so fast that you could hardly tell what was happening.

Her daddy knelt down and put his hands on Kit's bare shoulders. He was wearing his new maroon swim trunks and his terry-cloth shirt. He had on moccasins—I think he made them but maybe not. He was smart enough to make them anyway. He was afraid when he looked at the blood on Kit's leg. But he didn't scare Kit by saying he was scared. He wanted to make her feel safe so he said, "Oh, I don't think so. I really don't think so. You scratched yourself."

That's when a big thing happened. Kit just told her daddy about a very bad thing and he said it didn't happen. Everything started to get wobbly and thin. And the bottom of the cottage and the whole world and the whole universe split open and Kit fell through. First she tried to hang onto the chair and then her daddy's leg. But nothing was really strong anymore or really real, so her hand couldn't catch onto anything and she just fell into a big nothing. It was all empty and everywhere. It was much bigger than she was and much bigger than anything she had ever seen before. It was even too big to be afraid of. And she couldn't even tell if she was still falling 'cause there was nothing to look at. And she was there a long time.

But then she was standing on the arm chair. It wasn't real anymore but she was back in the cottage. And her daddy was saying, "You scratched yourself." And Kit was really mad 'cause she knew she didn't do anything to her*self*. And she knew her Uncle Ned did hurt her. Only, she also knew he *didn't* hurt her 'cause her daddy said so.

Her ideas couldn't fit in her head. And now she had a monster head with big teeth and bulgy eyes. And she was going to bite off her daddy's head.

And that's when another big thing happened. A big spider, so big that it had to bend its legs not to touch the ceiling, started walking toward Kit the monster. She turned back into Kit the little girl. There was no use in running away or biting off her daddy's head or fighting the spider 'cause it was gonna get her. She just stood there. And even though I'm magic and I'm friends with Kit and sort of am Kit, I couldn't do anything about that big spider. It just came over and picked up that little Kit and put its fangs in her and sucked out all her juice until she was empty. And it walked away carrying that empty husk of Kit.

Part V

AFTER REMEMBERING: WALKING IN THE WOODS

(1987-1990, Toby)

Your gentleness shall force more than your force
move us to gentleness.

William Shakespeare, *As You Like It*

The beaver chewed through the strands of the web
until the sun was freed.

Menominee legend

1. Toby and the Flappy Man

Three years after the cop punched her, Kit started seeing pictures in her head of that cottage at the church camp. The first time grown-up Kit saw Little Kit at the cottage in her mind, she didn't even recognize her. Little Kit was terrified and ran behind the umbrella stand and pulled it over on herself to hide. She always did that, even though it hurt. Big Kit didn't know who that scared little girl was. For days she kept seeing that little girl and wondering why she was thinking about her. It was like seeing someone else's home movies, and she didn't know why she had those movies in her head. It was like the movies were kept in a hot attic for a long time and they weren't in very good condition, so they kept breaking and then starting over, and sometimes the picture stopped and got wobbly and disappeared. She felt sick all that time and kept spilling cranberry juice all over herself. And when she'd start to see that little girl, flashing lights would get in the way so she couldn't see what was scaring her. And sometimes she'd get migraines.

Once she was with Georgia, looking at the wrinkled home movies in her head and telling Georgia about them. They kept breaking and burning and turning into flashing lights. And then, clear as day, there was this nice, tall man. He was wearing a suit that was a little loose on him. He said, "Hi. Can I help you somehow? I notice you're pretty upset. Is there something I can do?"

Kit told Georgia about the nice guy. Kit was smiling. There

was something kinda funny about this guy. He did a little dance and flapped his arms. Kit laughed. So did Georgia when Kit told her about it.

They all three talked awhile. The Flappy Man—that's his name 'cause of the way his arms and legs and clothes flap around when he dances—he didn't know anything about the Little Girl and the umbrella stand or anything. But he said he could sing and dance, not like in a movie, but real funny. And he did, and Kit and Georgia would get laughing and not worry so much about the Little Girl.

The Flappy Man kept showing up every time Kit started looking at home movies. The picture would fade or blink out and there'd be lights and then there he'd be. "Hey, can I help you with something?" he'd ask, smiling this real nice smile. He'd always show up when Kit was having trouble seeing the movies, and he'd try to help.

One day when this happened, Georgia suddenly understood something. She told the Flappy Man that she knew what he was doing, and that Kit appreciated how he had been protecting the Little Girl all these years, and that he'd done a good job of guarding the memories, but now it was time for him to let them out. Now Kit was ready to see those old memories that had been stored away for all those years.

First, the Flappy Man said he didn't know what Georgia was talking about. He tap-danced a little and said they could all go for a walk or sing some songs. But Georgia kept asking him to get out of the way and let Kit see the pictures.

He got more and more nervous. He stopped being funny and he stopped dancing. He told Georgia that she was a bad person and that she should leave Kit alone. Kit had to report all this to Georgia 'cause, of course, the Flappy Man was just talking in Kit's head.

Georgia didn't give in. She told him to step aside and let Kit see the movies. She said she knew it was him that broke the films and made the flashing lights drown out the pictures. She thanked him for doing his job so well for so many years and told him again that it was time for him to stop, though. At first she was nice. But when he started yelling at her, she got real strong and just told him it was time for him to leave and she wasn't afraid of him and nothing he did would make her and Kit stop trying to see the movies.

Then the Flappy Man said real low and threatening, "I'll give you a migraine." Kit felt sick. She was ready to give up. When she got migraines, she thought she might die. And sometimes she hoped she would. They hurt so much. It scared her when he said that, even though he was saying it to Georgia. To make her go away and stop trying to get the old movies out.

After that, the Flappy Man didn't try to be nice when he showed up. He'd just try to scare Kit and Georgia away from the movies. And Georgia would always tell him he had to get outa the way.

Georgia told Kit that the Flappy Man was a border guard, the part of her personality with the job of hiding the bad memories. She said she didn't recognize him at first 'cause she never met a friendly one before. Usually they're skeletons or huge rats or something scary.

Then one day Kit saw me standing by the screen door at the cottage. She looked surprised, like she never saw me before. I was half-way out the door, so she couldn't see me too well, 'cause it was bright outside compared to inside the cottage. I musta looked just like a short blob in front of the brightness. She asked me my name and looked even more surprised when I answered. Toby. She'd been asking the Little Girl questions, but the Little Girl was too scared to talk. She learned a long time ago not to tell people the big things. Kit asked me why the Little Girl was so terrified, and I told her it was 'cause the Bad Man hurt her. That's when she recognized me and Little Kit and started to remember some of the stuff. She got real sick for a while. Then she felt better. Every few months she remembers something else.

She also realized that Little Kit told her about this the first time Big Kit saw her, that time three years back with Georgia when Little Kit turned into the Orphan and the Goat and the Beast. Those weren't distractions. That was the message.

And she realised why she felt so yucky being counseled by her uncle and why she was so cold and sick that time she slept in "aunt Minnie's room" at the cottage. And she realized why her uncle made that hokey confession about the camp stool. But she didn't know if *he* knew why he felt so guilty.

Every so often the Flappy Man shows up and watches what's going on. He looks much older now and real tired. Too tired to dance.

Once he told Georgia that he was a failure. Either he failed at the one job he had, or else he wasted his whole life doing something useless. One or the other. Georgia told him he was good at what he did—protecting the memories. And now that job is over, and he could help Kit in other ways. Someone so lively and fun would always be good to have around.

Kit wasn't so sure she wanted him around, though. But Georgia explained that she had made him up when she was three to guard her memories until she was safe enough to look at them. The Flappy Man wasn't a *bad* part of her. It had lots of talents that she could use now in other ways.

One day Kit put on a tape of Nina Simone. She hadn't listened to it for a while. When Nina Simone started singing about Mr. Bojangles and about how he danced and "shook his clothes all around," Kit leaned over her desk and started crying.

2. Another Bear

One day Big Kit saw Little Kit while she was with Georgia. Georgia wasn't scared. She talked to Little Kit and gradually other things came into the picture with her. Little Kit was standing on a big bed. She didn't know where her clothes were. Suddenly there was a big hand reaching for her. Little Kit got scared and tried to back up toward the wall, but her feet got tangled in the sheets. Very quickly, Georgia said, "Here, you can have my spirit bear. It's very big and can protect you." That bear was in the picture before she finished talking. It roared like a rock slide and scared the big man away. It picked up Little Kit and she fell asleep in its arms, nestled into its fur. That was the first time Big Kit ever saw Little Kit relax.

Big Kit was real surprised about all this, especially that Georgia gave her the bear. Kit knew that Georgia had a spirit bear that was real important to her, but she didn't really know what a spirit bear was. It wasn't the kind of thing that she knew about or even really believed in. Later she said to Georgia, "I didn't know you could do that, you know, give away a spirit animal." Georgia said she didn't know you could either. It just seemed like the thing to do at the time. Kit asked if Georgia felt sad about losing the Bear. Georgia said it felt right, so even though she didn't know how, she knew everything would turn out OK.

Kit called her friend Dave and told him about the Bear, and then she walked up into the foothills to spend the night. There was a lot of wind that night and it felt real good to Kit 'cause it was warm.

She spent the whole next day walking and didn't get home till after dark. She went into her bedroom and there was the Spirit Bear sitting on the bed. It was huge and brown. It had claws. Kit was confused. Can ideas become solid? Or maybe she was crazy. She kept looking away and looking back. The

Bear didn't go away or get wobbly. It was really there. And the obvious thing to do was hug it, so she did. It was a good hug. If you visit sometime, I'm sure Kit would let you hug the Bear. Then she noticed a letter on the bed. It was a poem written by the Bear. Here it is:

I'll be here if you need me.
I'll keep you from all harm.
I'll help you scare away bad thoughts.
I'll even keep you warm.

You can hold me; you can hug me
When you feel a bit uptight.
You can hit or even kick me
If that makes you feel all right.

I know I seem a bit too big.
I take a lot of room.
But important things will find their space
As the child expands the womb.

Kit noticed that the Bear dictated the poem to Dave.

The next day Georgia dropped by. That was the only time she ever did that, coming over to Kit's cabin when they didn't have an appointment. She looked completely different. Her black hair was cut real short. She looked like a cat. Kit said there was something Georgia should see in the bedroom. Georgia looked at the bear and smiled and picked it up and hugged it. Kit said it was the Bear, maybe sorta checking to see if Georgia thought it was, too. And Georgia said, "Of course," like it was obvious.

"So, how did Dave know what it looked like? I didn't tell him." Kit was still trying to figure out how Dave knew some things that he shouldn't have any way of knowing. Georgia just smiled. She was more used to things like that. They didn't worry her.

Then Kit said she liked Georgia's haircut. Georgia said that after the session when she gave Kit the Spirit Bear, she suddenly wanted to cut her hair. She went straight to a hairdresser. Georgia and the woman talked a long time about all kindsa things. They didn't know each other, but they were interested in a lot of the same stuff, so they really got talking. Then the woman said she suddenly had an idea about how to cut Georgia's hair—they almost forgot about the haircut till then. Georgia said fine, she didn't have a special way she wanted it, she just wanted it cut. That's how she ended up looking like a cat. When she got home after that, she had a big urge to sit down and close her eyes. She barely did that and a black panther jumped outa the forest in her head. Georgia laughed 'cause it was like the panther was saying, "Well, it's about time you got rid of that Bear!" Kit laughed, too, when she heard about it. She pictured the Panther waiting around in the jungle for the Bear to leave. "It was time for Cat Medicine for me," Georgia was saying, "and the hairdresser figured it out before I did." Georgia had a new spirit animal.

3. Another Trapdoor

Kit pulled a rocking chair over to the wall and stood on it to reach the trapdoor in the ceiling. Then she looked at her feet and thought it was a pretty wobbly chair. She moved it away and got a ladder. She went up to the hole in the ceiling and tested the edges with her hands to make sure she found a strong part and then slowly climbed up.

Up there in the dark attic she stopped and thought about it. She went up in that hole a lot to put things away or get them out, but that was the first time she ever got something strong and tall to stand on. And that was the first time she moved her hands around the edge till she got to the part that didn't wiggle. She smiled. She knew trapdoors are good places for accidents, but she wasn't going to have one this time.

4. Thick, Heavy, and Sharp

Kit was lying in bed. She had this thick, heavy, sharp feeling. She couldn't move. As usual, she wasn't sure if it was her or something else that was so heavy. She kept trying to get air inside her. Finally she took a deep breath. She still had that thick, sharp feeling but she didn't think it was stupid. She thanked it for helping her remember.

Now she knew that bad things started happening to her before she knew how to talk—that's why it was so hard to describe this feeling—and before she knew that she was separate from the rest of the world—that's why she could never tell if it was her or something else that was so heavy.

5. The Rotten Orange and the Map

Kit sat in the maroon easy chair in her friend Dave's living room and clenched her teeth. She didn't like being yelled at, so she stomped outa the kitchen and plunked down in the chair. She was mad. It didn't seem fair.

After a while Dave stomped outa the kitchen and plunked down in the other maroon chair. They weren't yelling anymore, but sometimes they glared at each other.

Finally Dave asked why Kit yelled at him and she said 'cause he yelled at her and he said he yelled 'cause she was being mean. They were just like little kids. They stopped talking again.

Then Dave said in a different voice, "What happened?" That was a real question, not an arrow disguised as a question.

Because it was real, they both started thinking about the answer. They worked backwards 'cause that was easiest. Dave plunked in a chair. Before that Kit plunked in a chair. That was after she yelled at Dave, "Don't yell at me!"

"And I yelled at you because you told me I was wasteful," said Dave.

"And I said that because you told me to throw away that orange."

"It was rotten! You'd make yourself sick eating that orange."

"It was not! And don't tell me what's good for me and what's not!" They were sort of beginning to argue again. "I was willing to cut off the soft end and eat the good part."

"And be a martyr!" shouted Dave.

"Not at all. I don't *care* if the end is soft! You do. You eat the ordinary orange and I'll eat the good part of the one with the soft end."

"Because you'll make do." Dave's voice sounded all prissy and like a goody-goody little girl. *"You'll* eat the bad orange so the rest of us can have the *good* ones." Kit didn't know why Dave said "us" since there was only him. He was sounding stranger and stranger. "You'll be the martyr, or *play* the martyr, even though you have your own stash of cookies in the kitchen which no one else can eat."

Kit was real confused now. She didn't have any stash of cookies. She blurted out, "Who are you talking about!?" It was just the right question even though Kit didn't even mean it. She just said it 'cause she was confused and angry.

Dave stopped talking for a second and then he was crying. Kit could barely understand when he said, "My mother. She always used to do that." Turned out Dave's mother made a big show of sacrificing for her children by taking the burned toast or the bruised apple. But then she'd sit in the kitchen and eat whatever she wanted, even food that she never shared with the kids. Then she'd whip them with the dog chain if they peaked at her or said anything or tried to get some of the food when she wasn't there or even for no reason at all. Sitting there in the maroon chair, talking about the orange, Dave started to remember all that stuff.

Kit noticed that she didn't like the part when Dave told her not to eat the orange 'cause it was bad for her. She didn't like being told what was good or bad for her. Her uncle used to do that—and he was wrong. Now she didn't believe anybody who told her stuff like that, and she got real mad.

When they were done talking about it, Dave and Kit felt fine. They weren't mad at each other anymore and they both learned something. This was real different from their old arguments which just went on and on and never really finished. Those times, they just stopped and still felt mad at each other. Maybe arguments weren't so bad if you find out what they're really about, like mothers and uncles, not oranges.

"I know *that!*" Kit's voice shouted at Sarah. It scared both of them. Nobody said anything. Kit just drove the car, pretending to be busy watching the road. But she was thinking about why she did that. Why did she yell at her best friend when she didn't do anything wrong? She thought about the rotten orange with Dave and knew people don't get upset for no reason. And if they get more upset than you think they should, then the reason is probably a real old one. It probably doesn't have to do with the orange or the map.

The map. What happened? Kit was driving. Sarah had the map. They were driving through the desert in Arizona. They'd been exploring new places they never saw before. It was fun. They camped in some real old lava and explored big tunnels, real big tunnels, in the lava. They were big enough to hold maybe four trains on top of each other. But you could never get a train down in there 'cause it was hard to climb down there. Then they hiked in canyons and looked at Anasazi ruins. The Anasazis were Indian people who used to live around there a long time ago and build houses in the cliffs. Then they visited some teachers Kit knew on the Navajo Reservation. Then they were driving through the desert going home to Colorado.

And that's when the thing happened with the map. Kit asked Sarah which way to go at the fork and Sarah said toward Rock Point and Kit said—well, actually she yelled—"I know *that!* Which way is it?"

Kit wasn't sure why she yelled, even when she thought back about it. She was trying to do what she and Dave did with the orange. But she couldn't figure it out. What she could do was notice how she felt. She felt mad at Sarah. She felt like someone was thinking she was stupid. But she knew Sarah didn't think that. It was just a feeling. When Sarah told her to go toward Rock Point, Kit got that feeling. "Of course I know that, I'm not stupid. But which is the way to Rock Point? Do I go left or right?" As far as she could get in figuring it out was that she didn't like people thinking she didn't know something that she *did* know. She didn't want people to think she was stupid, but she wasn't sure why that was so important or when she got so worried about it.

They'd been driving along without talking a long time. Then Kit said she was sorry and she'd been trying to figure out why she did that. She said she knew Sarah didn't do anything bad. She said she knew it was about her past and she explained what she'd been thinking about and that she wasn't sure how being stupid got started as such a big worry.

Then Kit thought of something else. They'd been traveling together for two weeks, sharing everything, never being apart. And Sarah was Kit's best friend. Maybe, Kit was saying, she was suddenly scared 'cause she was too close to Sarah. She kept people at a certain distance. And maybe this was just as close as she could let somebody come. Maybe she got scared and pushed Sarah away.

Sarah thought that might be true. But you just don't yell at people like that no matter what. Kit thought that was right, but she didn't know how she could keep from doing something like that when she got scared again. She couldn't promise never to do it 'cause it wasn't something she'd ever *plan* to do. She didn't plan to do it *this* time, it just came out without her permission. She was worried, 'cause she knew stuff like that could come out anytime and she'd have no control over it—probably just how her uncle felt.

The only thing she could do was keep remembering and letting out her feelings with people who weren't scared by them and probably she'd do bad things less and less. That was all she could think of to do.

6. The Sliding Board

"That's your arm," the teacher was saying, "no one else's. Keep your eyes closed and let your arm just hang at your side. Feel what it's like. Let it move if it wants to. It's yours." Kit felt strange. Her legs were turning to water. If the teacher said that one more time about it being her arm, she knew her legs would be completely liquid and wouldn't hold her up.

"Please don't say it again," Kit was thinking as she stood in the room with the other students. "Please don't say it. I'm at the top of a long sliding board, and I'll shoot down into the past with no way to stop if you say that one more time. I'll be completely lost, gone from this room, back in a room with my uncle if you say it. It'll be embarrassing and I won't be able to control myself. Please."

Kit was taking a class in Trager body work. Trager is this way of touching people sorta like massage therapy but different. It feels good and helps you relax. A friend at folk dancing told her about it a year ago and said it might make her back better. Kit was pretty worried about letting people do stuff to her back 'cause it always felt dangerous. But she decided to try it, and Phil, the man who did Trager, never even touched her back—so she stopped feeling scared. It was when she was having a Trager session that she first started seeing the pictures of Little Kit. So she thought it was real good 'cause it helped her remember old stuff. And it made her back feel better even though Phil never touched it.

The part about her back was funny 'cause she didn't notice it was getting better till one day she hurt it by lifting a ladder. She thought, "Wow, this is like the old days when it always felt like this." That's the first she noticed that it didn't always hurt anymore.

Anyway, she decided to study how to do Trager so maybe she could help other people feel better, like Phil helped her.

But now the students were all standing there noticing the feelings in their own bodies. Their arms right now. And Kit was trying to stay at the top of the slippery chute. It was like the sliding board on the playground between the church and the parsonage after Kit and her brothers slid down it on waxed paper. It was scary 'cause you went so fast. Her brothers said it was fun, so Kit thought it must be fun even though she only noticed that it was scary.

"Feel it. Listen to it. It's *your* arm." And Kit went zipping down the sliding board.

After a long time, or maybe it was a short time, Kit knew she was curled up on something and shaking and making absolutely no noise. And it was dangerous to open your eyes or to breathe in the bad air or to breathe out and make a noise. And her body wasn't hers except for a hard nut deep inside her center under where the bones come together in front. And it was real important to save that 'cause it was all that was left.

Then she noticed her toes were wiggling and pushing against something. She was lying on her shoulder and it was getting hot. But the rest of her was freezing. She thought prob'ly she had ice inside her instead of blood. She was shaking a lot.

Then she heard a woman's voice, like maybe it was there a long time like a river flowing by but you just start to hear it after you've been standing there awhile. Then there was a blanket over her.

After a while, Kit remembered she was in Trager class. She was lying on the floor. The class was going on as normal. The teacher, Gail, was talking and it sounded like she was showing them some ways to work on people's sore arms. No one seemed upset. They were just letting Kit have her flashback on the floor. Flashback. That's what it was. She could tell the person who was sitting next to her, so she wouldn't worry.

It took a long time after that, but Kit finally opened her eyes. She was gonna explain what was happening. But she didn't say anything because she was so surprised. She wasn't where she fell down. She was all the way across the room, pushed up against the wall, with her head under the radiator. There was a woman sitting next to her just talking low. She didn't look worried, so Kit forgot about explaining. She was thinking about her wiggling toes pushing against the floor and realized that that's how she got under the radiator.

After a while she felt like getting up. She thanked the woman who sat with her and talked like a river, and then she joined the class again.

When Kit told Sarah about it later and said she was worried that she could have a flashback anytime, in the grocery store or the bank, Sarah said, "But you didn't, you had it in a safe place, with people who understood and weren't frightened." Sarah said wasn't that great? No one freaked out and called the men in white coats or told Kit to stop or drugged her. People do that kind of thing to people who are remembering, she said. And they say it's for the other person. But it isn't. They do it because *they're* afraid, because they can't handle seeing someone do something they're too scared to do. "But you didn't have your flashback around people like that. And I don't think you will." And Sarah was right. Kit had lots of flashbacks during the next couple years, but she never had one in the grocery store. And once she made room for them to happen at home or with a good friend, then they hardly ever surprised her anymore.

Except like the time when Sarah put her finger in a hole in Kit's pant leg and asked her if she thought she needed new pants. Sarah, Dave, and Kit just finished cutting some branches off Sarah's cottonwood tree and they were standing in Sarah's kitchen drinking water. Then Sarah noticed the hole in the knee of Kit's corduroys. Moving real quick like an elf, Sarah bent over, put her finger through the hole, and tickled Kit's leg. Kit's hand locked around Sarah's wrist before Kit knew what it was doing. I'm sure Sarah was trying to get her hand out 'cause she knew that Kit was about to go down the slippery chute. But Sarah's struggling felt like an attack to Kit and she couldn't let go. At last Sarah got her hand outa the torn pants, but Kit's hand kept hanging on. Suddenly Kit started crying and tried to run down the basement stairs. But Sarah stepped in front of Kit and wrapped her up in a warm hug. Only a tiny scary feeling came up and then Kit relaxed into Sarah's body and cried.

Something Kit really liked about those two friends was that they didn't mind talking to ghosts from out of the past. They didn't get nervous or have to leave when Kit went back in time like that. They stood around in the kitchen for quite a while comparing their ideas about what just happened. Kit guessed that her own finger poking through the hole in her pants wouldn't make her panic. It didn't. She also thought that if she was wearing shorts, her knee wouldn't be ticklish even to someone else's touch. She rolled up her pant leg and tested that idea by letting Sarah tickle her knee. No reaction. It was having her clothes invaded, not the actual tickling, that upset her.

Dave said what seemed best to him was that Kit reached out for a hug after the scare. Both Sarah and Kit knew that Kit was really trying to run away. It was easy to understand how Dave thought it was something else, though, since Kit headed for the stairway which was behind Sarah, and Sarah just stepped toward her instead of getting outa the way. But Dave thought there was more to his jumping to that conclusion. He said he wanted so much for Kit to be able to ask for physical comfort, not just to accept it, that he'd seen it where it didn't exist. They all learned something about themselves in that kitchen.

Another time when Kit was driving by herself, she got all the way to the chorus before she noticed what song was going through her head, "Trumpet Vine."

You came when you were needed.
I could not ask for more
than to turn and see you walkin'
through the kitchen door.

Those words brought the tears leaking outa her eyes. She was surprised 'cause she was feeling better than usual until just then. She pulled off to the side of the road and slid down the chute. After a while, she came back to her body in the car by the road in Colorado. And she was fine.

Another time, Kit went to a women's support group meeting. In the middle of the meeting, when they put on some music and everyone just moved around however they wanted, Kit got scared and curled up on the couch. The other people started gathering around her to see if she was OK, 'cause she was crying. They did a real normal thing, but it was the worst thing they coulda done. They touched her and talked about love. Kit couldn't talk or move. She just shivered and cried. She couldn't remember the piece of paper in her pocket which said, "YOU CAN LEAVE." She always carried that to remind her that she didn't have to stay somewhere where she was scared. She even wrote down the signs that meant it was time to leave: dizziness, flashing lights, nausea, trouble breathing, goose-bumps, shaking, confusion. But, of course, the signs got in the way of remembering the note. She'd also written down ways to leave a little bit, like going to the bathroom or stepping outside for a minute, or just backing up. And if none of those gave her enough room, then she could leave for good. But she couldn't remember those ideas or the piece of paper that had them written on it. After getting home later that night, she thought, "How am I supposed to prepare for the next situation where I am smothered by well-meaning people? The first thing to go is my mind. How am I supposed to remember the strategies I've worked out for the next time I lose my memory?"

But mostly it was like steam. If she took the lid off every so often, then the steam didn't build up and blow it off when she was in the grocery store. Kit felt sorry for people who were forced to keep their lids on and then got taken to a mental hospital when they blew off.

Kit thought about crazy people she heard about and nervous breakdowns. And she started thinking she was the same, only she was mostly around people who weren't afraid of her memories or her shaking and everything. And they used different words. Georgia said she was having a nervous break-through. And no one was trying to stop her. They knew that the only way to the other side of the forest was through it.

7. The Cocoon

For a long time—it mighta been about a year—Kit felt like she didn't *do* anything. She took the first Trager class, but then she stopped. Mostly she just sat in her big chair and looked out the window at the hillside and the draw. She didn't go on walks much. She left her great job. She was getting real skinny and throwing up and having diarrhea and she couldn't work. Actually, that was happening before she got her memories. Almost as soon as she quit her job, she started to remember. Maybe her memories were sorta like Georgia's Panther, waiting in the forest till there was room for it.

Kit noticed that she felt the worst just before she let herself remember. It was like holding back the memories took all her strength. The dam was falling apart, so it was harder than ever to keep back the water. And it was scary 'cause she knew she was gonna get washed away when it finally broke. She looked at people she knew and noticed that they got the stiffest about some idea right before they changed their minds. It was like the last battle and the old way fought as hard as it could before being killed.

So, Kit was sitting around a lot. She'd forget to eat. Sarah would call her up and say she saw snow on Mt. Audubon, did she wanta go cross-country skiing? And Kit would say no, she was tired. And Sarah would ask what she ate today. And Kit would realize she didn't remember to eat anything. And then she'd realize she didn't have any food and she was too tired to go buy any. Sometimes Sarah would say go buy a chicken and put it in the oven. But she never did. Once Sarah said what store to go to and she'd meet her there and Kit went.

That's when Kit realized she never cooked a chicken before. And when she touched it and started to wash it off she knew why. It made her sick to look at that slimy skin around the hole where you put the stuffing in. She remembered hating to watch her mother stuff a turkey or a chicken. But she also *had* to watch. She wanted to watch, but it made her sick.

She also remembered a time when she was walking along a sidewalk in Washington, D.C., when she was about 15, and suddenly there was a fight. A fat lady carrying a paper bag got knocked down and a raw chicken spilled out on the cement. Then a big man beat up the skinny man who knocked down the fat lady. The skinny man fell on the sidewalk, and a circle of blood under his head got bigger and bigger and touched the chicken, and then the chicken was in the circle with the man's head. Suddenly Kit heard a policeman asking her what happened. Maybe he already asked her a couple of times before. And she realized people were shouting. But all she knew was that the chicken and the man's head were in a pool of blood.

Sarah invited Kit over to her house and she'd just happen to have some fish and rice and broccoli. Sometimes it was too hard to get up and put her shoes on and walk down the path to the car and drive over to Sarah's, though.

Most days, Kit would have this experience. She'd be walking to the sink for a glass of water or heading for the bathroom and she'd suddenly realize she was gonna be asleep in about ten seconds, no matter what. And she'd throw herself toward the couch, which was cushions on a board on melon crates, and she'd be asleep when she got there. Later she'd wake up and feel like a cobweb.

All this time, she felt useless and like she wasn't getting

better and like she wasn't doing anything. When she told her brother Nash she felt bad about not working, he said he didn't know anyone who worked as hard as she did.

One day, Dave brought her a drawing from a magazine. It was really three drawings in a row like a comic: two pictures of a cocoon and then a picture of a butterfly coming outa the cocoon. Under the picture it said

"TAKE YOUR TIME AND DO SOMETHING WORTHWHILE."

Kit put a thumbtack through the paper and stuck it to the rough wooden door, where she could look at it from her big chair.

Georgia always reminded her that healing is a process not a product. That reminded Kit of a day in preschool. She was prob'ly four years old. It was clay time. Each little kid got a blob of gray, squishy clay. They played with it on a table covered with oil cloth. I don't know why they call it oil cloth, 'cause it isn't oily. Little Kit made a turkey outa her clay. Then she chopped the head off and the feet and scooped out the guts. Then she used the clay that used to be the guts to make stuffing and she put that back inside the turkey. Then Kit put her turkey in a pretend oven and sat in her chair waiting for it to cook. She was just ready to take it outa the oven and cut it up for the pretend family to eat when the teacher said time to clean up, put your statues on the windowsill to dry. Kit looked around the table for the first time and saw dogs and cats and people with hats and a snake. She looked at her turkey which wasn't really in an oven. It was just sitting on the oil cloth. And it wasn't a turkey. It was just a lump of clay, just like what she started with. She was wrong. She hadn't made anything after all. She smashed her turkey before anyone looked at it, and said she didn't wanta keep her animal.

But now Georgia was telling her it was OK to stuff a turkey instead of make a statue. Sometimes you have to do something like that. And it's OK if it takes a long time.

Kit has real good friends.

Once she was saying she didn't want to go somewhere with her friends 'cause there'd be other people there and what would she tell 'em when they asked what she did? Sit in a big chair and shake and gasp for breath? People suggested other answers. "I'm on sabbatical." "I'm taking time to re-evaluate and re-direct my life." "I'm a writer." That one seemed silly 'cause she wrote for herself, not anyone else. Her favorite answer, although she knew she couldn't say it, was "I'm doing what you wish you could do."

8. More Magic Trees

At Christmastime that year when Kit was mostly just sitting in her chair, her friends asked if she was going to do the usual thing she did and invite them to her cabin to make gingerbread cookies to decorate her little tree. That was the same tree A.J. gave her when she was six.

Kit thought about what shape the cookies could be that year. Since she moved to Colorado, she started doing a different shape each Christmas. It started as a mistake. Back in Virginia, she always borrowed her mother's gingerbread-boy cookie cutter. The first year she made cookies in Colorado, she got the dough ready and invited a couple friends over and then she realized she didn't have any cookie cutter. So that year they made up all kindsa shapes: animals and people and flowers and stars and everything. The next year Kit got a cookie cutter and they made gingerbread boys. It was nice to see that old friendly shape that she remembered from the first year she had the tree. The next year, they made gingerbread birds, all kindsa birds decorated with different-colored icing. The year after that was when Georgia gave Kit the Spirit Bear. So, the obvious thing to do was to make gingerbread bears. They were great. Some were fat and some were skinny. There were a few baby bears. One bear was walking sideways. Another one was clicking its heels.

One guy stood back from the tree and said, "Man, did I have fun. I don't usually do things like this. We should do this again." Kit thought that depended on what you meant by "this." If they did exactly the same thing again, it wouldn't be very much fun. The magic wasn't exactly what they did but that they allowed themselves to invent something, allowed the time "to evolve organically." That's what Kit said. In fact, she was thinking, it sounds like a great way to live. Make it up as you go along, with the people you're with.

So, as soon as Kit thought about what shape to do this year she knew it would be gingerbread butterflies. And that's what they did. They made cookie cutters out of the metal edges from waxed paper boxes. And what was neat was that you could change the shapes each time. So they had all kindsa butterflies. They even put some caterpillars crawling along the branches and a couple cocoons hanging down.

The day they decorated the butterfly tree, Kit thought she might be beginning to come outa her cocoon. A.J.'s tree was still magic.

9. Nuts Aren't Hummingbirds

The first time was about the telephone. Well, the first time that it was a problem.

Dave and Kit were boyfriend and girlfriend till she got her memories. Then they were regular friends, but real good regular friends. It was Dave's idea. Kit kept having flashbacks. Dave liked being Kit's boyfriend but he asked her if it would be better not to have a boyfriend. And she said yes. Kit was relieved but also sad. She wondered if she was so messed up that she'd never have a boyfriend again. But after a while she stopped worrying about that so much.

There was a part, though, that did worry her. Besides flashbacks, Dave said she also had "disdain." I'm not sure what that is, but it's this thing that Kit does when a person, especially a man, likes her a lot. When he said that, Kit knew right away that it was true and she knew that it wasn't the first time she did it. It was just the first time someone saw what it really was instead of thinking it was something wrong with him. Seeing this herself for the first time and knowing she always did it really scared Kit. She didn't know how she could ever stop it 'cause it was automatic, and she already did it and made the man feel like a bad person before she knew what she was doing. But she had so much other stuff to think about right then that she set that one aside for later.

So, about the telephone. Dave called up one morning from his house in a town about 15 miles away. His voice sounded tight and angry. Suddenly he asked Kit why she said those things last night to her friend in Idaho. Kit was confused. She got a call late at night from this friend. They talked for a while. But how did Dave know that? "All I know," said Dave, "is that your voice woke me up in the middle of the night. You were saying to Luke that you loved dancing with him."

That was true. And it was fine for Dave to know that. But *how* did he know? Kit felt dizzy and sick. Her legs curled around each other. And she felt a hard knot in the center of her. She heard a little girl's voice in her head saying real fast, "I don't know I don't know I don't know I don't know," like a chant to keep something bad away. Kit was feeling like she had no private place, not even inside her own head. She felt like Dave was magic and could come into her head when she didn't want him there. There was no private place. This was worse than when the kids stole her journals. At least she could just not write things down if she didn't want them to know them; she could keep them in her head. But how could she stop thinking? Dave could hear what she was thinking or saying on the phone miles away.

Dave was feeling awful, too. He couldn't go to sleep in his own house and be sure that no one would wake him up in the middle of the night by talking in his head. They both felt sorta invaded. They were both scared.

The next time was a little different 'cause it wasn't about a telephone. Kit drove to Denver so her friend Lars could help her fix her concertina 'cause one note just played all the time by itself. By the time they were done, it was late and there was a lot of snow. So, Kit slept on the couch.

In the morning, Kit woke up 'cause she heard Lars talking in the kitchen. He'd say something like, "You sound pretty upset." Then he wouldn't say anything for a long time. He was talking on the telephone.

After a while, Lars came into the living room and asked if Kit wanted to talk to Dave. Dave *was* upset. He woke up in the middle of the night again and saw Kit lying on the couch in Lars' living room. Some of the picture was clear. But some of it wasn't, like he wasn't sure if Lars was on the couch, too, which he wasn't 'cause he was in bed. Dave was saying he thought Kit didn't *want* a boyfriend. And she was saying she *didn't*. She just wanted to drive home in the daytime since there was so much snow. But she had trouble talking at first 'cause her mouth wouldn't open and there was such a hard knot under where the bones come together in front and she was dizzy. Finally, the three of them decided to meet at a restaurant in Boulder in an hour.

By that time things didn't seem thin and wobbly to Kit anymore and she didn't feel sick. She was thinking it was great that they could have a misunderstanding and decide to get together and talk about it, even though it was a little scary.

They ate omelettes—which is stuck-together scrambled eggs—and talked. And what was weird was that they told the truth. Dave asked Lars if he wanted Kit as a girlfriend. And Lars said sometimes he did. Lars asked Kit if she wanted to be his girlfriend. And she said no but she liked having him as a regular friend to go backpacking with and play music with. Then Kit asked Lars why he left her when they used to be boyfriend and girlfriend a few years ago. He said he didn't know. But he wondered if things would be different now that she had her memories. He asked Dave if being Kit's boyfriend was better now. Both Dave and Kit laughed and said that it got so bad that they weren't going together anymore. Lars laughed, too. Turned out they all had this idea that everything would get better for Kit right away when she remembered the truth. Kit was suddenly thinking about touching the hummingbird. She thought: some things happen faster than you expect and some things happen slower.

Then Kit thought of something else. When she started having flashbacks with Dave, she said to him once that it was pretty weird and a new experience. He said not so weird and not new either. There were those other times like that when she'd shake and cry and kick and curl up. Kit laughed 'cause she knew she never did that before. But Dave was sure she did. She was sure he was thinking of an old girlfriend. Finally, Dave told her the story of one day, how they went walking in the mountains and ate lunch and everything and she ended up shaking and curled up. Kit recognized the story except for the end. But she had this funny feeling in her stomach when she heard about it and gradually she thought he was probably right and she just forgot it.

Suddenly there in the restaurant she thought, "I wonder how many other things I forgot. I know I forgot a lot of my childhood. And it seems I forgot later things, too." She turned to Lars and told him about the experience of forgetting things with Dave. She asked him if she ever acted that way around him—shaking and curling up and crying—although she knew she didn't. And he said she did. So, it was true. Maybe she did lots of things she didn't remember, even when she was grown-up. That was pretty weird to think about.

Well, by the end of the omelettes, they'd said a lot of true stuff and they felt real good. And it wasn't scary after all, although they all thought beforehand that it might be.

But Kit and Dave kept having this other problem—it was a problem for both of them—of Dave seeing and hearing Kit even when she was far away. They asked Georgia if she could help and she said sure. But Kit couldn't imagine how she could. They got together and talked a little and Georgia said that Dave and Kit responded in opposite ways to being hurt as children. Dave learned to expand, so he could pick up signals from people from a long way off. This way, he could get out of the way before that person started hitting him—which happened a lot anyway 'cause he had to be at the table for dinner and in his bed at night. He had no choice about being some places. Anyway, Kit did the opposite. She contracted—that's like shrinking—until all she was, the only part she protected, was the little hard nut in her center. The more scared she got, the smaller and harder that nut got.

Georgia had them do experiments. They closed their eyes and each of them pictured a sort of private balloon to be in. Then Georgia had Dave grow his balloon out until Kit said she could feel it touch her balloon. Kit thought this was pretty weird. The only reason she was willing to try it was that, even though she didn't understand how, she had to admit that Dave knew stuff about her that he shouldn't be able to know. So, Kit was only partly surprised when she felt pushed against, even though Dave was about two meters away. She just waited till she felt uncomfortable, like someone was getting in her way. That happened when Dave's balloon was pretty far inside Kit's muscles. That's where the skin of Kit's balloon was. And as soon as she felt it, her balloon started to shrink. If his kept growing, hers would go all the way down to being a little nut. Kit felt sick and cold when that happened. She hated it.

It reminded her of when she hired another teacher to help her on the workshops in Indian schools in Oklahoma. As they drove hundreds of miles from one school to another for a whole two weeks, Kit got sicker and sicker. Being in the car was the worst. She felt like she was suffocating. She could feel a big pillow pressing on her face so she could hardly breathe. Now she understood. She was a "contractor" trapped in a small space with an "expander."

After having Dave get big, they tried the other way. Kit was s'posed to get big. It was harder for her. But finally she grew her balloon till it bumped into Dave's. He got the hang of it real fast and he could grow and shrink real easy. Kit was slower.

For days Dave kept checking his balloon to see how big it was, and it was always enormous, bigger than Colorado. But he could shrink it down to human size whenever he wanted. After about a week, he said that he got his automatic setting to be just a little bigger than his body. Now when he checks, that's how big he is. But he can change anytime he wants to.

Kit tried to re-set her boundary to be bigger, but it was hard. Sometimes when she checked, it was the size of her body, but sometimes it was little. And almost every time she got scared, it shrank to a nut. Not everything is like hummingbirds. Some things take longer than others.

10. Walls

A friend invited Kit to spend Thanksgiving weekend with her. Betty and her daughter and Kit would rent a cabin in Utah and go hiking in the desert canyons. At first Kit was excited—she loved the canyons—then she felt bad about it.

Sarah asked Kit what felt bad and Kit didn't want to think about it. Then Sarah asked what would happen when they got to the cabin, and Kit said they'd set their bags down and Betty would say, "Why don't you and I share a room, Kit, and let Becca have the single room. I'm sure she doesn't want to be stuck with her old mom." And then Kit wouldn't be able to say anything but OK. The problem was that Kit was feeling real private these days. She knew she wasn't very good at making what Georgia called boundaries. She felt like she needed real walls to protect herself since she didn't have very good walls inside herself. Her balloon was too little and too weak. So, that was it. She wanted a room of her own in the cabin in Utah and she thought she couldn't have it.

Later, she talked with Dave about it, and he said why didn't she just tell Betty. Kit never thought of that before, and it was a real scary idea. Dave said to try saying it to him for practice and Kit couldn't even do that. Dave said they could try it with him being Kit and Kit being Betty. That way was easy. It seemed real natural when Dave said he needed a room of his own because he was feeling so insecure these days. Finally, they tried the conversation with Kit being Kit. They had to practice it a buncha times before she could do it without shaking.

When Kit finally told the real Betty, not Dave pretending to be Betty, Betty said fine. And that was all there was to it.

11. Another Knock-Out

Even before the big man ran toward her, Kit fell down and started crying. When he jumped on top of her, she saw a light that hurt her eyes and she felt cold and sick and dizzy and she couldn't breathe. And then she was swinging with me in the air. A few minutes later, she ran to the edge of the room and fainted. But when she opened her eyes, she saw the big man knocked out on the mat and she heard the other women cheering.

Kit was taking a special self-defense course for women. It was called Model Mugging 'cause they do like a model of a real mugging. She found out that her legs could learn the kicks and do them even when her mind went away to play with me. Sorta like the old days in the cottage, but then her body just lay there and got hurt and now it fought back.

During the first class Kit got so sick she couldn't drive home. Her friend Betty, who was also in the class, took Kit home with her and sat up with her while she threw up in the living room. Kit threw up most of the night. After a while it was just the water Betty gave her so she wouldn't have the dry heaves.

Every time Kit practiced fighting in the class, she went back to being a little girl and being scared by her uncle at the cottage. Then one time she decided to do it on purpose. She asked the male instructor to act out a time she remembered. Kit decided she'd let her uncle think she was a two-year-old but secretly she'd be her forty-year-old self and surprise him. She didn't really know if she could do that 'cause so far she always felt like a little girl when she got attacked.

The man pretending to be her uncle put on the big helmet that protected his head from the kicks. He already had on the rest of the suit that made him look so huge and fat. But he didn't wear it too look fat. He wore it so he'd be safe inside when the students kicked him with all their might. Then when he felt the kick that woulda knocked him out without the special suit, he'd pretend to be knocked out. That way, the students learned how hard you have to kick to make someone stop attacking you.

Then they acted out the scene Kit remembered. The big man held her hand and they walked into the pretend bathroom. He said he'd help her take off her bathing suit so she could take a nice warm bath. But then he pretended to pull down his own swim trunks. He said, "Do you know what this is? Would you like to touch it?" Kit's whole face curled up and I thought she might forget to stay grown-up. But she didn't back up and hit her head on the pipes under the sink the way she did when she was two. The big man kept coming toward her and then he grabbed her shirt and suddenly she realized there was a man trying to hurt a little girl and this wasn't the time to think about him. It was the time to protect the little girl. She yelled, "Don't touch her!" They had a big fight but Kit's mind never went away. She gave him the kick that woulda knocked him out. Everyone cheered.

For the rest of the class, whenever Kit got attacked, she stayed grown-up and protected herself. She didn't feel sick or dizzy or see a light that hurt her eyes. And she stopped thinking it was always her uncle. Seemed like when she did it on purpose once, she didn't have to do it by mistake anymore.

That was the first time Kit noticed she was angry at her uncle. Before that, she knew she was scared and sick and dizzy and a buncha stuff.

She also understood about how her uncle could get so mixed up that he would do those bad things to her. She found out from her aunt that her uncle was hurt like that when he was a little boy. It made sense. He was hurt and had no one to tell, no way to show his feelings. So those feelings of being scared and sad and angry sat 'way inside his body and kinda rotted, and the poison from the rotting leaked through him and made him feel awful and ugly and bad and unloved. (Kit knew how that felt. When she was little she always had a devil inside her. She could see it and hear it. It had horns and a tail and said mean things. Now she thought the devils in people were the pain they never got to talk about.) Kit knew that Ned wanted to feel good and loved. And one way he tried was by holding Kit and touching her with that grown-up type touching.

Anyway, Kit understood all that about how if a person's feelings can't come out in the regular way, they get pushed down and then they come out sideways. They just break through and squirt out. She knew that about herself and her uncle. They were alike in having squished feelings rotting inside them and making them feel bad. And the more they pushed them down, the more they broke holes in the feelings container inside them and came spouting out making a mess all over themselves and the people around them. Like throwing the scissors at your father or yelling at your best friends about the map or the rotten orange. Those rips in the feelings container and the poison that squirted out made them feel sick and made them do things that no one understood, not even them. And she knew it wasn't the feelings that were dangerous but the squishing them down. And she knew she was feeling better and better the more she let them out through the regular faucet instead of letting them rip up her insides.

So, like I was saying, Kit knew about this stuff, she understood some things about her uncle. But it wasn't till that day in the self-defense class that she knew she was angry. She knew from talking to other people who were hurt as kids that people do these things in different orders. Some people got angry first.

For a long time after that, pretty often at first and then later not so much, she kicked the wall of her cabin—she put a pillow there so she wouldn't hurt her foot—and screamed at her uncle. After a few months, she was finished. She just didn't feel like doing it anymore.

All that time, though, she thought it was kinda weird. She understood why her uncle did that stuff. He was abused himself. She understood and felt sorry for the hurt little boy he was, for the hurt little boy who still lived inside him waiting to be noticed, listened to, protected, loved. She understood but she was also angry. She decided those two things weren't opposites. They could live side by side in her.

"And anger isn't the same as blame," she thought. She was angry, but she didn't think it was his fault. She didn't blame the people who abused *him* either. "Just like my uncle, they acted out of their own torment, the unexpressed anguish from the abuse they experienced. Blame and fault are useless concepts when looking at something this big."

She decided it wasn't a matter of bad people hurting good people. She saw a picture of all of us caught in the same invisible web. As we jerk around to get away from the strings that are holding us, they tighten on us and on everybody around us. "The random, frantic struggling increases our own pain and passes it on to others. Some completely different type of movement is needed."

Kit thought about Trager. When you do Trager and you find a stiff place, you don't push harder, you back away. That part is tight for a reason, 'cause it feels scared. So, instead of scaring it more by pushing hard, you help it feel safe by getting real gentle or even not touching it at all. Sometimes when Kit did Trager she'd find a leg muscle, say, that was hard like a rock. Once when she felt a muscle like that, she just set her hand on it and didn't move at all. In about a minute, that muscle suddenly turned soft and the man started crying like a little boy who was real sad. Lots of times when a muscle relaxed like that a feeling would come out, too.

Kit thought a lot about how Trager worked, getting the movement the right size so it wouldn't be scary. She thought that was probably the only way to get out of the invisible net, too. Stop thrashing around making everyone more scared and hurt. And just slowly search with your hands for where the strands are holding you and gently jiggle them free.

And the best part is the more you untangle yourself from the web, the looser it is for everyone else.

12. Prayer Sticks

At the end of the self-defense course, all the students were gonna give each other little presents. They were gonna get together after the last class to do this thing of giving presents. Kit didn't know what to give. She really liked the other women in the class and wanted to give them something good.

She was sitting one day in her big chair, looking out the window at a flicker eating ants. She was thinking about how all the women in the class had some trouble with the religion they were brought up in. They were all different, Catholic, Buddhist, Jewish, Protestant. And they all did different things about their religions. Some of them switched. Some of them stopped. Some of them stayed. But everyone seemed to want to talk more to her own spirit part, if you know what I mean. Maybe you don't, 'cause this stuff is hard to put in words. But anyway, they all thought they had a special spirit part that was hurt or hidden when they were little. And they wanted to let it out again.

Kit just read a story with prayer sticks in it. She never saw a prayer stick. She didn't know what they looked like or how big they were or anything. But once she heard that a prayer stick could actually be a prayer, you know, it would be the same as the words. She heard that a Navajo prayer stick could mean the words, "With beauty above me, with beauty below me, with beauty all around me, I walk in beauty." A person told her that feathers from a sky bird and a ground bird meant the first part about above and below, and that beads around a cord meant the last part about beauty all around and I walk in beauty. She was looking at the flicker again. Then she thought about the dead flicker that Sarah gave her for her birthday. Kit still had the wings and some other feathers. She decided to make prayer sticks, not Navajo prayer sticks 'cause she didn't know what they were like and, besides, she's not Navajo. And maybe she wouldn't call them prayer sticks. That word "prayer" always felt kinda yucky. But anyway, she'd do something with sticks and feathers that had to do with finding that spirit part.

She cut up some chokecherry sticks and tied some dried weeds to them. "With beauty below me," she thought, even though it was weeds and not feathers. Maybe she'd use those words anyway. She liked them. Even though they were a prayer, they didn't say anything about the Lord or sinners or stuff like that. They just talked about beauty, which Kit knew was more than just being pretty. It was like having things straightened out and balanced. She liked that. Then she tied a string to the stick and put some beads on it and tied flicker feathers to the end. Each breast feather had a tiny heart on it. That was good.

Then she made some outa mountain mahogany twigs. She didn't tie weeds to them 'cause they had their own decoration. When the flowers are done, the petals fall off and leave a little, fuzzy curly-cue behind. It's about an inch. The mountain mahogany twigs had those pretty curly-cues all over them. She kept changing how she made the prayer sticks, so they ended up all different. But they all meant the words: "With beauty above me, with beauty below me, with beauty all around me, I walk in beauty."

After the last class, all the students came up to Kit's cabin and gave each other gifts. There were daffodils and poems and moon necklaces and sage bundles and lots of other neat stuff. And then they all sat outside in Kit's big hammock from Mexico and the hook broke and they all fell down and laughed.

13. Sharks' Teeth

The women in the self-defense class liked each other so much that they decided to keep meeting after the course was over. The teachers weren't there, and they didn't practice fighting anymore. They just got together to talk and have fun about once a month. If there was a holiday around that time they'd think of a way of celebrating it together, their own special way. Like, when it was Easter time, even though some of them weren't Christians, they each brought something that reminded them of spring or new life or starting over. Some people brought flowers. Someone brought eggs. Another person brought a poem.

At Thanksgiving, everyone brought food to share. This was different 'cause they didn't usually eat when they got together. Some of them were overweight or afraid of food or had some other problem about eating. So they decided not to include food in their getting together. Also, there's this idea that the only way you can have a party is to eat, and they wanted to see if they could have a fun time that didn't depend on food. And, anyway, most of them had kids and had to cook everyday, and it was nice to do something that didn't make them have to cook more.

But at Thanksgiving they decided to try including food. They knew they could have a good time without it. They'd proved that to themselves. Now they'd see if they could have a good time that included food. It turned out great. People ate what they wanted and they talked about their problems with food if they needed to.

Someone brought a candle to put on the table. A couple people brought poems. At the last minute, Kit picked up some sharks' teeth to bring to her friends. Before they started eating, Kit let everyone choose a shark's tooth. A couple people wanted more than one. That was fine. Kit had lots of them from back when she and A.J. used to collect them on the beach. Kit said that teeth are important 'cause they help you protect yourself from danger and they help you take in nourishment. They could all keep those sharks' teeth to remind them that they could do both those things—protect themselves and nourish themselves.

14. Maya Angelou

Sarah gave Kit a book by Maya Angelou. It's called *I Know Why the Caged Bird Sings.* Kit said she read it before, a long time ago, but she'd like to read it again. It was Kit's mother, Ruth, who lent it to her years ago.

Kit started reading the book, but the weird thing was that she didn't recognize it until she got to the part where Maya gets raped when she's a little girl. Kit remembered that part exactly. It was the only part of the book she remembered. Hm, that's interesting. Kit wondered if her mother knew something about what happened to her without really knowing.

After reading that book, Kit bought all the books Maya Angelou wrote and read them all. Maya Angelou became Kit's hero. She was a woman who got hurt and not only survived but learned how to thrive. That's what Kit said. Then one day Sarah said that Maya Angelou was coming to town to give a talk. So, Kit and Sarah went two hours early to get good seats in the front row.

The talk was wonderful. And the way Ms. Angelou moved was as good as the way she talked. Sometimes she seemed like water. Sometimes she seemed as strong as a mountain or as dangerous as a snake. She could be an old woman or a little girl or anything she wanted.

After the talk, there was a party that anyone could go to. People stood in line to talk to Ms. Angelou. Kit stood there for a few hours, and when there was only one more person in front of her, a woman said that Ms. Angelou was tired and had to leave. Kit was so disappointed she started to shake. She was thinking for hours about what she wanted to say to Maya Angelou. She had a little speech ready by then, and now she couldn't say it. Then Ms. Angelou stood up from the chair where she was sitting and looked at all the people still wanting to talk to her or get their books autographed, and she sighed and stood there a few minutes. Then she said no, she couldn't leave. She'd stay until everyone there got to talk with her.

The girl in front of Kit got her book signed and then it was Kit's turn. Kit knelt down by the table in front of Ms. Angelou 'cause she knew her voice wasn't strong enough to come down from her mouth to where Ms. Angelou was sitting behind the table. Suddenly Kit couldn't remember anything she wanted to say and she started to cry. For a while she couldn't say anything. Maya Angelou stood up and said softly, "Come here." And she held her arms out. Kit walked around the end of the table and stood next to Ms. Angelou, who is over six-feet tall and big and powerful. Ms. Angelou's arms wrapped around Kit and held her against that big, warm body. Kit cried a deep cry that wasn't about being afraid. It was about being safe. After a while Kit stopped crying and just felt Maya Angelou breathing. Then they let go of each other and just stood there. Ms. Angelou asked if Kit wanted her books signed, and Kit said no, she got what she needed.

15. Slippery Memories

Sometimes Kit would remember something bad that happened when she was little and then later she'd forget it again. Once she told Sarah about a big hand grabbing Little Kit in the bathtub. Later, Sarah said how it made sense that Kit was afraid of bathtubs. Kit wondered why Sarah thought that. Sarah said 'cause of the time you got grabbed in the tub. Suddenly Kit saw that picture again in her head. But till Sarah said that, she forgot completely about it. Sarah said that didn't surprise her. After all, Kit spent most of her life hiding those memories from herself. It was a new thing to remember them. It would probably take quite a while before the remembering got more automatic than the forgetting.

One day Kit was talking with her brother Nash on the phone and suddenly she knew she was going to tell him about her memories. She didn't make a plan about how to tell her family, but she knew she would sometime. She didn't try to hurry it. She just waited till it felt right. And this was how it started, on the phone with Nash. He listened and cried. He didn't tell her it wasn't true or that she should forget about it because it happened a long time ago. That was a good phone call.

But that night Kit woke up suddenly and remembered what she told Nash. Sitting there in bed, she couldn't imagine why she made up that story. She felt terrible and she knew she had to call him right back and tell him it was all a mistake. But first she called Sarah. Sarah wasn't surprised 'cause Kit always did that when she told her memories to someone important. She'd call up Sarah and say she made up a terrible story about being hurt by her uncle and she didn't know why she did it. Right then Kit wouldn't remember that Sarah knew all about her memories. She'd tell Sarah this stuff like she never talked to her about it before. And Sarah would always be real calm and say no, she didn't make it up. Those things really happened. She was sure of it. She'd say, "I look at you and the way you act and I know you were abused." Sarah would say that people don't act that way for no reason. And a healthy person wouldn't have to make up a story about how she was hurt. An unhurt person wouldn't need to comfort herself with a story like that. That's not a story, Kit, she'd say. It's what happened to you.

But Sarah said that she knew Kit had to forget or deny it sometimes when she got scared. And that was OK. She could forget as much as she needed to to feel safe. And she didn't need to worry that she'd convince Sarah that it didn't happen. She *knew* what happened. Sarah said Kit wouldn't be all tight and controlled the way she was if she hadn't been hurt. And she wouldn't faint in Model Mugging class and throw up. Or scream and cry and try to run down the basement stairs when Sarah tickled her leg through the hole in her pants. "I *know* you were abused," Sarah said. You can deny your memories all you want. I'll hold them for you."

Kit decided not to call Nash back after all. And later that day she started remembering some of the stuff she forgot. Oh yeh, the bathroom in the cottage, her uncle pulling down his swim trunks, the big hands holding her in the Bad Bedroom, the light bulb hurting her eyes.

After a few weeks, Kit went to visit Nash and his family in Vermont. While she was there she told Nash that she wanted to tell their parents but she knew it would be awful. She knew just what would happen. She'd get on an airplane and fly to Virginia and go to their apartment and tell them her memories and they'd either cry and say it was their fault or try not to cry and tell her it was a long time ago and she should forget about it or tell her she needed psychiatric help or a drug so she would feel better and get rid of her crazy ideas. Then she'd get on a plane and go home to Colorado and everyone would feel bad.

Nash sat there for a minute. Then he said, "Or *I* could get on a plane and go tell them the story. Or we could go together. Or you could send a tape or a letter. Or I could take them a letter from you. Or they could go to your place. Or you could all come here. Or we could think of some other plan."

Kit was amazed. She thought she knew the only way that story could turn out. But Nash came up with a bunch more ways in just a few seconds. She didn't make a decision right then. But the stuck, stiff feeling she had about telling her parents was gone.

One day after she was back at home she woke up and started making a tape for her parents. She just suddenly wanted to do it. She told them her memories and how they started coming back to her. At some places she cried.

When she was done, she called Nash. They worked out a way that everyone in the family could get a copy of the tape and hear it with someone who already knew the story, someone who could help them, whatever their reactions might be. Kit knew she didn't want to be that help person. She had too many of her own feelings to deal with. She knew she couldn't help other people with theirs. Kit got the information to her brothers and cousins first. Then she sent tapes to her parents and her aunt. Nash went to be with Ruth and Bill when they got their tape.

The night after Kit mailed the tape to her parents, she woke up in the middle of the night again and did the usual thing of forgetting all her bad memories and wondering why she sent that crazy tape. Sarah helped her again and reminded her that after spending nearly 40 years keeping those memories buried and making up a whole story about how they couldn't be true, she was pretty good at doing that and it was hard to turn off the automatic part that kept trying to bury the memories. And she also said that it was OK to do that and that Kit shouldn't worry about losing the memories forever 'cause Sarah would never forget them.

When all Kit's relatives heard about her bad memories, they

all seemed real surprised. But before Kit told them who did those things to her, they all asked the same question: "How did your uncle Ned have the chance to do that?" Which was weird, 'cause she never said anything about her uncle or what the man looked like who hurt her.

16. The Red Fish

About a year later, in August, Kit and her aunt and her cousins and her brothers and their partners and children all went to the cottage at the camp for ministers to celebrate Bill and Ruth's 50th wedding anniversary. Kit's parents said they could do it somewhere else if it was too scary for Kit to go there, you know, where most of the bad memories were. But Kit wanted to go there. She asked her big brother Nash to go early with her so she could get used to the cottage before all the other people arrived. She thought more memories might come back or something, but nothing important happened. And then the rest of the family came.

All Kit's relatives were there. Well, not all of them. Her uncle wasn't there 'cause he divorced Kit's aunt and married someone else a few years ago. He didn't have anything to do with Kit's family after that. Everyone knew about Kit's memories, and they all told her how brave she was, and some of them asked her to help them. Sometimes people cried and sometimes they cooked corn on the cob and mostly they had a lot of fun.

One day Kit's brother Scott and her dad were carrying a big mirror through the living room to take it upstairs to hang on the wall. But before they could get to the stairs, everyone started playing with the mirror. Someone could stand at one side and put the mirror edge right down the middle of his body. People at the other edge saw a whole person, only half was real and half was a reflection. You could get really crazy-looking things if the person at the end stood on one foot, the one the other people couldn't see, and held the other foot up. That way, the lookers saw a person with a real foot and a reflected foot both off the floor and it looked like magic. You could also get one big eye or no eyes or two heads or one arm connected to both shoulders. Or you could mix up a couple people and get all kindsa arms and legs tangled in one. That was one of the best games the family ever played. They did it and laughed and fell on the floor and did it some more. The grown-ups and the children were all doing it and laughing.

One day when just the two of them were sitting on the eating porch, Kit's mother told her about something she remembered a few months after hearing about Kit's memories. It was about taking Kit to the doctor for a check-up when she was real little. Kit's mother remembered that when the doctor looked between Little Kit's legs, Kit looked terrified. Then the doctor said, "The hymen has been ruptured. Do you know how that happened?" Kit's mother didn't know and the doctor quickly went on to something else and said, "That can happen... with active play." Kit's mother heard that calm voice that didn't fit with the look on Little Kit's face and she tried to feel OK, even though she didn't know what those words meant. What kind of active play would do that?

When big Kit heard about this, two things happened. One was that she thought the whole world musta been afraid to know about this sorta thing when she was little. Probably most people still were. Otherwise, why were doctors taught to say that stupid thing about active play? And why did her mother let the doctor's voice calm her down? And why did her mother forget about that for 40 years and not remember it for months after she heard Kit's story? And why didn't her father go upstairs and ask her uncle what was going on when she came running down the stairs bleeding?

But the first thing that happened when Kit heard about the doctor was that a part of her said inside her head, "It really did happen!" That was the first time Kit knew that there was still a part of her that didn't believe it. Well, now it did.

Kit's mother told her another thing that Kit never heard before. When Ruth was 13, she went to live with her aunt and uncle 'cause her parents didn't have enough money to feed both their daughters. I guess this sorta thing was common then. Ruth was in 9th grade. She did her homework at the kitchen table and her uncle would help her with her algebra. He did this by standing behind her and leaning over her shoulder. His hand would rest on the chair and then move out to point at something on the paper and then it wouldn't get all the way back to the chair. It would just kinda come back to the edge of the table and rest accidentally against Ruth's front. Then it would point at something else and come back and flop down on Ruth's shoulder and dangle there against her chest. It would move around a little to get itself comfortable. This felt creepy to Ruth. She didn't like it. When she explained this to Kit she said, "Now, it wasn't anything like what you experienced. That was horrible! But I think it's odd that we both had a bad experience with an uncle. But what happened to me wasn't sexual abuse. I didn't know what sex was." Kit said that, of course, she didn't know what sex was either when she was a baby being hurt. "You don't have to know what sex is to be sexually abused. You were abused," she said.

"Oh, I don't know," said her mother. "And anyway I took care of it." Kit was excited. Her mother told someone! Good for her. But that wasn't it. "I just got in the habit of slumping in the chair and sliding my body completely under the table and sitting right up against the table edge so he couldn't touch me."

At first Kit was disappointed. But then she thought that was all the taking care of that her mother could do. Her aunt and uncle were giving her a place to live and good food to eat, so she couldn't complain. But Ruth still didn't think she was abused. Maybe she couldn't take that in yet. She was still working on taking in the part about Kit.

Kit thought about 13-year-old Ruth squishing under the table, and trying not to let her front show when she stood up. Then she thought about 75-year-old Ruth with her crippled, crooked back. A doctor once came into an exam room, looked at Ruth standing there, and then walked back out 'cause he knew that was the wrong person. He knew the person whose x-rays he had wouldn't be able to stand up. But those were Ruth's x-rays.

Different people left on different days. By the end of a week there were only a few people left. The day before Kit was gonna leave, she was up in the bathroom looking for a bar of soap in the old oak wash stand. She opened the drawer and suddenly got all shaky and cold.

She picked up what she saw in the drawer. It was a clear, hard plastic ball for children to play with in the bathtub. Inside it were some little chips of colored plastic and a red plastic fish. They rattled when you shook it.

Kit was real surprised to see that fish again. You see, she had forgotten about the ball, but she saw that fish a lot when her bad memories came back to her. But when she got those memories she didn't think about the fish much 'cause it seemed so weird to see a stiff, red fish when you were remembering being hurt. But suddenly there it was, the fish she saw in her head all the time, the fish that never fit into the story and always seemed a stupid thing to be thinking about. Now she knew why it was tangled up with those other pictures. She musta held onto that ball and let her mind go inside it and stay with the fish when she was being hurt in the bathtub. Of course, when she got hurt in the bed, I'd come get her and we'd go up through the ceiling.

She took that ball and went downstairs. Her mother was the only person there and she knew right away that something unusual was going on with Kit. All Kit could say at first was, "I remember this fish." Kit's mom said she could have the ball and do whatever she wanted with it. She said Kit could smash it if she wanted. Kit held the ball real tight and said, "No, that's where I went to be safe." Kit was crying. Then she told her mother all about the ball and seeing the fish in her memories and not knowing until now why it was there. "I would never have known, if this ball had been thrown away. There must be lots of other things that I won't ever know because the clues are gone. Maybe it doesn't matter, though. I know enough. Some people don't have any clues except what's in their minds and their bodies." Then she cried some more and even though she was 40 years old, she sat on her mommy's lap and they both cried.

That night at dinner, people were talking about education and Kit said one of her ideas about school feeling like prison for some kids. Her father was clearing the dishes when she said it and he looked down at her and smiled and made a very little noise of air coming out his nose. If you were watching, you could tell he was a very nice man and you could tell he didn't agree with Kit's idea. You could tell that he thought it was a silly idea not worth talking about, or maybe it was an idea he was afraid to talk about, one or the other. Suddenly Kit tried to scream, "It's true! It's true!" But her voice was so blocked up and tight that it came out like a squeak. Then Kit ran away from the eating porch.

Later, she went into the kitchen, where her father was washing the dishes. She said, "I'd like to tell you what happened for me then." He said that would be fine. She said,

"I told you something—it was even something about children feeling trapped—and you dismissed it. That's what..." Kit started crying and could hardly talk. "That's what you did when I was three years old and told you Uncle Ned hurt me. You dismissed my experience as not worth talking about."

After Kit was crying less, she said, "I can understand why you had to do that. You dismissed my experience because it was too frightening to face. What I was telling you was probably quite literally unthinkable for you. There was no place for that thought in your world. It would threaten your view of your family, your brother-in-law, your religion, the whole world. I can understand why you couldn't think that thought. But I felt tonight as if it was happening again. I was trying to shout at you, 'It's true. It's true.' That wasn't about tonight. That's what I've been trying to say ever since I was three years old—by having accidents and being sick and all of it." Kit stopped. Her father wasn't washing dishes. He nodded his head and said, "I understand." And he didn't smile or make a little noise of air going out his nose.

The next morning when Kit was packing, her father came out on the sleeping porch and tried to say something. "I want to tell you... It's been hard for you... Coming on this trip... Here in... Where..." It was the first time Kit ever heard her father have trouble with words. He was a minister and could do a good sermon anytime. It was scary hearing him talk like this. He wasn't in control of his voice the way Kit was used to or the way he was used to. He finally said, "What you said last night. I understand. You're courageous." His face wrinkled up in a way Kit never saw before. Of course, he was crying. But Kit took a couple seconds to figure that out. It was scary.

But a lot of scary stuff happened the past few years. And Kit noticed that every time something new came out it scared her, but then she felt much better and it stopped scaring her. And that's what happened with her father crying, too.

On the way home, Kit thought about courage. She didn't feel courageous. She just felt like she was doing the only thing she could do. She was lucky to have real good help and then things just opened up. In the opposite way, her uncle was unlucky 'cause he didn't have good help. Probably that was true even when he was a little boy. Little Kit was luckier than her uncle 'cause she was in a family that really did love her even though they couldn't hear her big problem. And she was lucky when she was a grown-up to meet people who could hear her even though her shouting was all in code by then and even she didn't know what it meant.

Maybe courage was as useless a word as blame. Courage was just being given the tools you need to do something hard. Yeh, it was a gift. Not being given the tools didn't make you bad. It just meant you were stuck in the net with the cords cutting you and with your thrashing making the cords cut other people.

17. Cornered by Another Good Man

The little cabin looked so safe and warm. Kit had been away for three weeks and she was real tired. She went to visit some friends and then to see her parents for the first time in over two years. It was their 50th wedding anniversary. It was a good trip but Kit was real tired. All she could think about was how good it would feel to be alone in her safe little cabin.

Her stomach kinda jumped in a sick way when the big man stepped out from behind the cabin as she put the key in the lock. She knew him. He was her favorite professor back in college 20 years ago. He was the smartest person Kit ever met, and he always helped her in college. But now he grabbed her and hugged too hard. Suddenly she couldn't see his face. They went inside and Kit set down her bags. She could barely think, but she knew somehow it was important to tell Cliff that she was exhausted and desperate to be alone. It was hard to make her mouth work, but she told him. Cliff said he understood and wouldn't stay long. He told her about how he got the idea to drive the thousand miles to see her and how he was learning to recognize and accept his feelings. He read love poems and told her awful stories from childhood. Kit thought it was great that Cliff was learning about these things, but she couldn't handle it right then. She told him again that she was "emotionally drained" and needed to be alone. She said she couldn't have one more intense conversation. He said they'd keep it light and then started crying about his mother.

The whole time, Kit was having trouble seeing Cliff's face. It kept wobbling and then fading away. His voice was like that, too. Sometimes she could hear and sometimes she couldn't. Then he asked if she didn't want to change, if she wouldn't like to be able to accept love from a man. Kit was so dizzy and sick that she could hardly think. He was right. She did want to get better. She did want to be able to accept love. But she felt attacked and her stomach was a knot of barbed wire. She knew she had a problem with men but she also knew she wanted Cliff to leave.

Each time Cliff asked for something, Kit did what he asked, hoping that when he got what he wanted he'd go away. That may seem weird—trying to get rid of someone by being nice. But Kit learned to do that when she was real little and her uncle wanted to do bad things with her. Doing those things was the only way she could think of to get him to leave. So, she let Cliff read "one more poem" about ten times. She got him tea and bread. She lent him a sleeping bag for his trip. But he wouldn't leave. Each time she said yes to a request, she added, "And then I simply *have* to be alone." And Cliff always said something like, "Of course. You must be exhausted. I'll leave right after this poem."

More than seven hours later, Kit stepped out the door and said she would walk Cliff to his car. It felt like a rude thing to do, right in the middle of his talking. He kept sitting in the big chair for a bit longer and Kit almost felt too embarrassed to keep standing outside. She was just about to come back in when Cliff came out. When they reached the bottom of the hill, he said, "Oh, I have one more poem in the car. Hop in and I'll read it to you." The idea of sitting in a crowded car with this excited man was so scary to Kit that she finally said the magic word: "No." And she walked back to her cabin without saying good-bye.

For two weeks, Kit kept an eye on the path to her house and worried about Cliff coming back. She started sleeping at Sarah's house so she wouldn't be home if he came. She was furious that her cabin wasn't really hers. Even when she was there alone she didn't feel alone. It was like there was a ghost there, right inside the place that was supposed to be safe. And it felt dirty. She couldn't use the chair Cliff sat in, even though it used to be her favorite chair. And she couldn't move the pile of poems off the table. Her favorite mug was dirty and she couldn't get it clean. Even the air felt contaminated. She was afraid to breathe it.

One day, Kit saw the fawn who was born behind her cabin in June. Cliff had said he enjoyed the fawn as he sat behind the cabin waiting for Kit. Sometimes when men say they enjoyed something, Kit felt sick and she felt sorry for the thing they enjoyed 'cause it might be hurt or used up. She thought about that poor fawn being enjoyed. Then she thought about how Cliff went to the post office to find out where her cabin was since it wasn't on a street and how he walked all around asking people where she lived until he found it and then sat there until she got home. She thought about all the times she said she simply *had* to be alone and all the times he said yes. She thought about how he said he'd keep it light and then he'd tell her about marital problems and how he loved her and he'd cry.

She looked at the fawn and suddenly she felt like a deer herself, a deer being hunted. Suddenly she was sure that she wasn't rude to make Cliff leave. She knew that he had treated her the way her uncle used to, and for the same reasons. Not because he was bad but because he was so full of his own needs and an idea that he was helping her that he couldn't hear what she really needed.

She grabbed a bundle of sage (the one that was the present from the woman in Model Mugging), set it on fire, and went outside to cleanse the fawn like she'd seen Indian people do with sage smoke. Later, she thought it was kinda strange that the fawn let her do that. She took the sage inside and smoked the chair and the table and the poems and the mug and the air. It took a lot of smoke to make the house hers again. She'd never done that before, cleaning with sage smoke, but it really worked. You could say that the smoke cleaned the cabin or that the idea of it cleaned her mind, but it's the same thing.

But the cabin wasn't really saved. While the sage burned, a man and a boy pounded in surveying stakes. One of them was right where the fawn had been. They put pink plastic ribbons on the stakes. Kit suddenly felt little and helpless. She felt foolish. Here she was trying to protect her cabin, and it was about to be torn down and all the little trees in the draw, for a man to build a mansion.

And then where would the fawns be born?

18. The Body Knows

Kit couldn't lie on her stomach. It hurt her back too much to do that. So she never did. That was a problem when she was studying Trager, that special way of touching people to make them feel better, 'cause half the work is done that way. She was afraid that she couldn't learn to do it if she could never have it done to her.

Also, she was mad 'cause she didn't understand why it should hurt to lie on her tummy. She always wanted to understand things, and sometimes she even thought something couldn't be true if she didn't understand it. But not so much anymore. Not since her body gave her the old memories that were too terrible for her mind to hold when she was a kid. And she had to admit that lying on her stomach made her back hurt, even if it didn't make sense, even if it should be the opposite. She always thought she should be afraid of lying on her *back* 'cause that way looks dangerous and because she got sick and dizzy when someone touched that soft place under her heart. But she was more afraid of lying on her tummy, even though it looks safer.

One day in a Trager class—Kit started studying it again—the teacher started talking about when the person rolls over so you can work on the back of him. He said, "When you pick up a person's leg when he's prone, his weight pivots on the sternum, opening up the whole core of his body." Kit could hardly listen to the teacher, it was so scary. She bent over and curled her arms up in front of her body. "It creates an irresistible stretching, lengthening, opening here," and the teacher pointed at that soft place under where the front bones come together, that place where Little Kit used to save a piece of herself when everything else was being touched and moved by her uncle.

Suddenly it all made sense. Suddenly Kit's brain knew what her body knew all along: lying on her stomach was dangerous. It made that secret place helpless. All someone had to do was pick up your leg and that secret center got stretched open. Kit felt sick just thinking about it, and she saw a picture in her head of a big hand picking up a naked little girl's leg.

Later, she laughed about how slow her brain was about understanding and how mad it got when it was left behind. Still, it sure felt good to solve that mystery. And she wasn't sorry she had a brain that liked to figure things out. It was real useful sometimes. It was just good to know that it didn't have to do everything anymore. Her body was smart, too, and had lots of information for her. And you know what? Kit could lie on her stomach after that, just a little at first, then longer and longer.

Another interesting thing happened in that class. The teacher showed pictures of horse and pig skeletons and then a person's skeleton. He showed how a person's skeleton had to be different to stand on its hind legs. One thing he pointed out was a curve in the low part of the backbone. "The lumbar curve," Dean said, "is part of what makes us human." Kit felt awful. She knew she didn't have that curve. She never did. Maybe she wasn't completely human.

Dean explained how a baby isn't born with a curve there. It gets that curve when it starts to walk. Some ideas started to come together in Kit's head. Her mind was figuring out something else her body knew a long time ago. Kit knew that she got hurt before she could walk or talk. She knew she never got a curve in her backbone and that her back always hurt even before that time at the boat house. She knew that her backbone started curving a little sideways when she grew a lot when she was about 14.

It all fit together. Her muscles clamped down when she was scared when she was a baby. Then they stayed clamped after that, which kept her bones from moving and growing the right way, which meant she never got the right curve and her back wasn't set up to work right for walking on her hind legs, so it always hurt.

Actually, she started feeling better when she figured that out. Especially when she realized that since she'd been getting Trager from Phil, her muscles were getting more relaxed and her back didn't hurt all the time. Come to think of it, Phil once said that she was beginning to get a curve in her back, just a little. She didn't think about it much at the time, but now she thought maybe it meant she was becoming more human. She was pretty sure she was.

One day Kit went to a different Trager practitioner 'cause Phil was away. She began to relax, turning her body over to the gentle movements. But then, after she had sort of given up control, she suddenly felt unsafe. The rhythm going through her body wasn't hers. It was like a soft invasion. She began to slip down the sliding board into the past. Fighting against everything she learned back then, especially that there was nothing that she could do to protect herself, she used all her strength to climb back up the chute, push her voice through her tight throat and whisper, "That feels dangerous." It was one of the bravest things Kit ever did, if you think about it. 'Cause she learned that complaining or telling about getting hurt could kill her.

But this practitioner didn't know that bodies can know things that minds haven't figured out. In a quiet voice meant to be reassuring, she said the worst thing she could have said: "No, this isn't dangerous." And maybe to prove to Kit that it was OK, she kept doing the thing that felt so frightening. I guess her mind "knew" that Kit's body was mistaken. She did just what Kit's father did when Kit was three. And probably for a lot of the same reasons. She denied Kit's view of reality because it sounded impossible and also because she didn't want it to be true. And Kit did the same thing she did long ago. She shot down the sliding board. She let go of her reality and left her body so that it could live through the experience.

Several days later, after Kit recovered from the replay of her childhood experience, she realized that she'd been given something useful. A good example of how she *didn't* want to do Trager. She told herself never to ignore or contradict what a client told her, even if it made no sense to her. And it wouldn't matter if the person told her with his words or with the way his body reacted. She must never ignore the message.

19. The Letter

Kit wondered if she'd ever get an urge to talk to her uncle about her memories. As the months and years went by, she thought probably it just wasn't on her list of things to do. She figured one of her cousins would want to talk to him. And that seemed fine to her. She told all her friends and family that they could tell anyone they wanted about her memories. It wasn't just that she didn't care, she *wanted* people to know. For one thing, she was tired of the family having this secret and it felt good and clean like water for it not to be a secret. Also, she figured if her story could help someone else, then it made all that bad stuff be useful. It wasn't just a waste then. Like A.J. giving her the already-dead snake.

But anyway, she didn't feel like telling her uncle about it. She didn't think he would like hearing from her. And she didn't think she'd like what he'd say to her. There was a possibility that it would be a relief to him, too, to stop keeping the secret. But that didn't seem very likely.

Then one day her cousin Rose told her about these kids who used Ned as a sorta grandfather. Maybe the way A.J. was like a grandfather to Kit. Suddenly Kit felt scared for those kids. Maybe she didn't need anything from her uncle. But maybe those kids needed something from Kit. She decided it was time to write a letter to Ned.

A long time before that, Sarah told Kit that she wrote a letter to Ned, and Kit could have it to send or re-write it or do anything she wanted with it. In it, Sarah said things like it was hard being a parent and she knew that she had hurt her daughter when she was little. All she could do now was tell her daughter what she did, so she would have the truth to deal with. Then she talked about Kit's memories and how she was getting help to get over those things. And Sarah said she hoped that the end of the secret was a relief to Ned and that he had someone who loved him who could tell him he was a good person and that he would get help in getting over his own pain.

So, Kit added some things to that letter to make it up-to-date and then sent it to her uncle. She also sent copies of it to her relatives with another letter to them explaining what she was doing. So they'd all have the same information, you know, and not be wondering who knew what. Sarah signed the letter to Ned and told him that Kit didn't wanta talk to him but that he could talk to her if he wanted. Then Kit and Sarah took it to the post office.

The next day, Kit called Sarah and said guess what, she just did something terrible. She didn't know why she did it. That sorta thing. She said that for some reason she wrote a letter to her uncle saying he abused her when she was little. This time she remembered that she was abused, but she had no idea why she told her uncle that it was him that did it. She couldn't think why in the world she said that. You see, she even forgot that Sarah was the one who wrote the letter and went to the post office with her.

Sarah was nice. She kinda expected this. She said there were lotsa reasons Kit knew it was her uncle. The memories were in his bed at the cottage and at a room in his house in Albany. And the man in her memories was fat and had doughy, white legs like her uncle, and he had her uncle's slow, deep voice that was strong and gentle at the same time.

And her aunt recognized the lamps and the windows in the room Kit didn't recognize in the pictures in her head. They were from a house Ned and Helen lived in a long time ago, when Kit was real little.

When Sarah said all that, Kit remembered. That was weird though. For a while she not only forgot the reasons she knew it was her uncle, she forgot that there were reasons. Sarah never forgot, though. Or Dave or Georgia or Kit's brothers or parents. They could always hold her memories when they were too slippery for Kit.

Oh, Kit's uncle never wrote back to Sarah. He talked to his kids, though, Kit's cousins. They said he was pretty angry—which isn't surprising. But Kit felt good that she had Sarah send her letter. At least now Ned's new wife knew that someone thought Ned used to hurt little girls. And even if she didn't believe it, maybe she'd just be a little more careful about leaving Ned alone with his "grandchildren," even if she didn't notice she was doing it.

20. An Open Hand

This was one of Kit's favorite times of year, when she went to the redwood forest in California and learned Swedish dances. Kit thinks Swedish dances are magic. I think they look like a ball that's heavier at one end. They do that sorta lumpy rolling. That's 'cause the men and the women are usually doing completely different steps even though they're dancing together, one woman with one man. I don't know how they keep from killing each other. Kit says that when it works, you get this funny feeling in your tummy, not like getting sick, more like floating outa the top of a tower.

When Kit woke up the first morning there in the redwood forest, she walked through the woods, under the huge trees, down to the river. She had a favorite place where the river curved. On the outside of the curve was a big rock cliff with moss and orchids growing on it. On the inside of the curve was a little beach with sand and gravel. Big trees grew all around and made shade almost everywhere. Up in those trees, thrushes sang a bubbly song that fit right in with the water noises.

Kit just walked to that place 'cause she loved its sounds and the deep, green pool under the cliff. As soon as she got there, though, she knew what she wanted to do. She took off her clothes and set them on the gravel. She walked into the pool and felt the clean water touch all of her skin.

She felt like she was Big Kit and Little Kit at the same time. Big Kit helped Little Kit wash all the dirty feeling off her body. It wasn't hard. She just stood in the pool and let the river flow past her. The water just swirled and slid by and took the old, bad feeling away. Kit could feel the dirt sliding off her legs and tummy and chest and back. Then she leaned back and floated in the water and let the current carry her around the bend to where it got shallow. It even felt like her brains got cleaned when she did that.

This was something Little Kit tried to do a long time ago and Big Kit tried to do it all her life, but she never could. All the places that are made for people to wash in made Kit feel dirty and sick. So the more she tried to get clean in a hard, white bathtub the dirtier she felt. But here in the river under the big trees, there was no white tub and no metal arm holding the shower head and no tile floor and no locked door and no walls to trap her. Here there was just the green river and gravel and tall trees that she could walk between and moss and the thrushes singing like water.

That night after supper, Kit sat in the cozy, log dining room with her friends and listened to the Swedish fiddlers give a little concert. The older fiddler was saying they'd play a special tune. The younger fiddler, his daughter, looked surprised and then tried to hide it. Gert said that he had been in the forest when "this tune came and I took it." They barely started playing when Kit began to cry, which was weird 'cause she was real happy.

The next day, Kit told Gert that his tune made her cry and then she wished she hadn't said that because he might think she was complaining. But he just said, "Good," and she knew he understood. She added, "It touched my deepest pain."

The next day, Gert asked her if she would tell him what she meant about her pain. She told him that she was sexually abused when she was a child, and then it was time for supper.

The next day, Gert came to Kit and he looked real upset. He said that he couldn't stop thinking about what she told him and that he'd been sick all night. They walked a long time under the huge redwood trees and finally he said that during the night he started remembering things from his childhood. At first he thought they were dreams, but then he realized they were memories. He cried a lot and said he didn't mean to tell her.

For the next two weeks, Gert kept telling Kit all the memories that came up. Sometimes he'd tell her he made a big mistake and he knew they weren't true. Kit recognized that feeling. She said he could doubt those things as much as he needed to. And he wouldn't have to worry that she'd doubt them. When she heard herself say that she thought, "So, Sarah really meant it when she said that to me." Kit always believed Sarah when she said that, she thought. Well, a little part of her must not have believed it.

Gert told Kit that he appreciated what she was doing for him, that he couldn't thank her enough. And Kit said another thing she heard from someone else. It was Phil who used to say it when she'd thank him for the Trager work. "I'm not doing anything. I'm just present while you're doing something courageous." Then she thought, "Why do I say *just* present?

It's true that I'm not doing anything, it's true that I'm just present, but that's a lot. That's just what a person needs when he's opening up a scary past. And it's not something most people can do—be present. I'm only beginning to learn how."

During the two weeks, besides talking with Gert, Kit danced a whole lot. And sometimes she got real silly. She and some friends made up some funny dances and got everyone laughing one night. While she was doing that, Kit saw the Flappy Man in her head. He was dancing and laughing like the first time she saw him. He didn't look old and tired anymore. I guess he found a knew job.

After two weeks of dancing, Kit drove back to Colorado. She'd never driven that far by herself, more than a thousand miles. The friend who drove out with her was going home a different way. In the middle of the night, she drove off the road and parked in the desert. She played Kôllåten on her concertina. That's the tune that made her cry. (Gert told her that until that night in the log dining room he hadn't played that tune since his father's funeral. That's why his daughter was so surprised.) Then Kit went to sleep in the desert.

The next day she drove the rest of the way to Boulder, through lots more desert and then over the Rocky Mountains. She was planning to sleep out one more night, but she was really excited about getting home, so she drove late to get all the way there.

When she walked up the path to her cabin, she saw a piece of paper attached to the door. It said she had to move out at the end of the month. That was just a few days away.

The man who wanted to tear down the cabin and all the bushes in the draw and build a mansion had run into trouble and wasn't able to do that. So, this note was a big surprise. Kit sat out back in the darkness, looking into the thicket and cried a lot. She'd been in such a hurry to get home, but she didn't have a home anymore.

Kit moved all her things into Sarah's basement and then slept on the couch in Sarah's living room. She spent a few months visiting relatives and friends, and a funny thing was that she was real happy. She thought she'd feel like a refugee or an orphan, but mostly she felt free. And she learned that she didn't have to be in her little cabin to keep healing. She could do that wherever she was. She also knew she wouldn'ta felt so good if she had to leave her cabin a month ago. It made a big difference that now she knew that her hard work with her memories wasn't just for herself. It could help other people, like Gert. Somehow, that made it easier to leave her cabin.

She didn't feel like a refugee. But during that time when she didn't have a place of her own she met some refugees. Her friend Nancy from Vance's address book (but now she was in Kit's address book, too) invited her to meet a Vietnamese family at the Denver airport. The man lived with Nancy's family back in the sixties when he was a student. When he went home to Vietnam, a lot of things happened. Two important ones were: he got married and he got in the big war that America was in. For years he was fighting and didn't see his wife much. Then one morning he woke up and everyone around him was running and jumping on helicopters in their underwear. They didn't even have shoes on. His friend said to hurry and jump on a helicopter 'cause they lost the war and needed to escape. But Tran didn't want to escape without his wife and baby so he just ran into the jungle. Of course, he got captured. For a while he lived in a cage too small to stand up in. Other times he lived in different kindsa jails. He was a prisoner for 8 years. All that time, Nancy's family wrote letters and made phone calls to people who try to get prisoners free. They found out where he was, but it took years to get him out. Then he found his wife and daughter and they were happy to be together, but they were all sick and didn't have any money. Nancy's family spent the next 7 years trying to get them to the U.S.

That night when they finally got there, Nancy and her family and Kit met them at the airport. Tran's daughter sat on a plastic chair and her eyes looked somewhere that nobody else could see. Kit tried not to stare at her, but she thought a lot about what that girl's life musta been like, and what taught her body to go limp like that when she was frightened.

Even though they'd been traveling for days, Tran and his wife looked real happy to be in the Denver airport hugging Nancy's family.

Then they all went to the baggage claim area. There was a big pile of suitcases. Someone started loading the bags onto a cart. "No, just the two metal boxes," said Tran. Quietly he said to Nancy's mother, "Refugee luggage." He was sorta trying on the word like a coat. He'd been a foreign student and a husband and a soldier and a father and a prisoner. Now he and his family were refugees.

They were free, but they paid for their freedom. Kit thought, "Their world is gone, their possessions, their friends and relatives, the earth that contains the dust of their ancestors, familiar contours, smells, and leaf shapes that would always mean home and which they would never see again."

Kit looked at those two boxes. They were smaller than the apple box she used to keep her stones in. What was in there? And when did they lose their other stuff? Gradually over the years? Or suddenly when the war ended? They woulda lost their cooking utensils and clothes and furniture. But also grandmother's picture and the flute grampa played and the... Kit really didn't know what they used to have.

But she knew everything she had 'cause she just put it all in

Sarah's basement. What would she save if she could only keep what would fit in one of those metal boxes? Would she feel light or deprived if her stuff got taken away? She knew how heavy and awkward her stuff was. And she knew exactly how much she had—enough to almost fill up the spare room in Sarah's basement. How much would she miss it if it disappeared? Kit thought she'd probably miss it pretty much. "I'd feel bereft, not free. Am I a prisoner of my security?"

One of the places Kit stayed was with a friend who spent a lot of time "doing good for others." She made fancy food and took Kit to "places of special interest." She was very nice to Kit. But the odd thing was that the longer Kit stayed there the worse she felt. Her neck got stiff and her shoulder and back hurt and she felt nauseated but she didn't want to be ungrateful, so she didn't mention that and just ate the food. Kit didn't know what was wrong but she knew she felt like a bad person.

When she went to stay with her brother, she felt much better, more relaxed. And she could think again. She realized that when someone does things for you from duty it doesn't feel as good as when someone does things for you from love. In fact, it doesn't feel good at all. It feels awful. She thought about Indians and Africans being done good to by missionaries. She felt sorry for them. Being done to doesn't feel good.

While Kit was traveling around, Gert invited her to come to Sweden to co-direct a music and dance camp. It was a scary idea. But Kit had a test to figure out if she would do something she was afraid of. If she had a heavy fear like lead, she wouldn't do it. If she had a tingly fear, like your foot coming awake, she'd do it. She decided to go to Sweden in the spring.

She could do anything she wanted. She just figured that out. Not having a house helped. She had a picture in her head of a hand holding onto something valuable. That hand couldn't get any of the gifts that were showering around it. There was another hand that was open. Things fell into it. Sometimes they stayed there awhile. Sometimes they rolled off. That hand got to have lots of different, wonderful things. Kit felt like she was finally learning to open her hands a little. But she still thought she'd be pretty sad if she ended up with just one box of stuff in a country that had the wrong shapes and smells.

21. Summer and You're Packing

While Kit was packing up all her stuff to move outa her cabin, she noticed that a little pile of things was collecting in a corner. She knew it was the young part of her, Little Kit, who was making the collection, so she just let her do it and didn't bother her with grown-up questions. After a while Little Kit found a little wicker suitcase, real little, just big enough for her special stuff. Big Kit still didn't know what it was about. But Greg encouraged Kit to do whatever she needed in order to feel safe. And letting Little Kit collect her stuff felt safe.

Oh, Greg was Kit's new therapist. Georgia moved to Canada and Kit decided not to have a therapist. After a few months, she decided to get one again. So, she got Greg. When they had a session and Kit curled her legs together and curved her shoulders in and put her hand over her mouth, Greg didn't tell her to stop or ask her if she wouldn't feel more comfortable if she didn't do that—like her uncle did when he was being her counselor. You know how some people tell you you'd like something and they really mean they'd like it. In fact, he encouraged her to curl up as much as she needed to feel safe. He'd even help her if she wanted by using his hands to curl her shoulders for her—but only if she wanted.

Once she was sitting like that all curled up and with Greg's hands holding her shoulders. He spent a lot of time getting it perfect. He'd ask, "More pressure? Less? Is this the right angle? Let's give your shoulders exactly what they want. There's no reason to leave it only almost right. A little more down? OK." Suddenly it was perfect and her shoulders relaxed. They realized someone else was taking over for them. They didn't have to stay tense to protect Kit. It was being taken care of by someone else. It was like landing in that green meadow where it was safe and you could relax. Kit cried real hard for a long time. She felt safe and looked after, just like she wanted when she was little. And she could cry real loud without worrying about telling the bad secret. It wasn't a secret anymore.

After a while Kit started feeling cramped and hot all curled up like that. She told Greg he could move his hands and she unwound her legs and let her shoulders lean back against the chair. She felt relaxed and happy and warm. She always wished she didn't have to sit curled up with her legs twisted. But when she made herself stop, she felt sick and scared. But this time she stopped and she didn't feel scared, because she wasn't forcing herself to. Just like Greg said, if you feel scared and protect yourself, then you finally feel safe. And eventually your protections start feeling too tight and small and you want to take them away if there's really no danger. That's different from forcing yourself to get rid of them. That doesn't make you safe. It makes you more scared. Greg is real smart.

One of the last days Kit was in her cabin, she had a meeting there with Greg. The chairs were gone, so they sat on the floor. Suddenly Kit knew what she wanted to do. She needed to open the little wicker suitcase and look at what was in it. First, she pulled out the plastic ball with the red fish in it. She started crying and told Greg about the ball where she used to hide when bad things happened in the bathtub. Then she picked up a little red, cloth bag. Inside was a tiny stone bear that her friend Ellie got for her in Arizona, that time they went to the Yeibichai. Someone told her that a fetish—that's what the little bear is called—has the strength of the stone it was made of, the animal it looks like, the person who carved it, and the person who owns it. Kit thought it probably also had the strength of the person who gave it to her. She cried some more when she held the little stone bear.

Next she picked up a little framed picture. It was a tiny painting of a girl and a goat done on a leaf from India. The little goat had skinny legs like the goat that Little Kit turned into sometimes, and like the fawns behind the cabin.

Little Kit, inside Big Kit's head, said, "You don't have to play with all the stuff if you don't want to." Big Kit smiled even though she was still crying. Then she held up a bead necklace that a little boy made for her a long time ago. He was the headmaster's son of the school where Kit was a student teacher. He and his brothers and sisters always had to rush through breakfast 'cause Kit was trying to get to school at the same time as breakfast. The necklace had a flat piece of soapstone in with the beads. On one side Nat carved, "I love thee, Kit." On the other side he scratched a picture of an owl and wrote "guess who." But the who was in a bubble that meant the owl was saying it. That was how Nat always signed notes to Kit, so she knew the necklace was from him even though it didn't have his actual name on it. Greg said a child's love is special, and Kit was crying more. Next she picked up a screech owl wing. It was little and real soft.

Everything Kit took outa the suitcase made her cry: a tiny, dried-up jellyfish; a stone that looked like a picture of red mountains against pink sky; a postcard of a Mexican girl holding a baby. They both looked real sad. Kit could see these were all important things, but she still didn't know why

Little Kit put them all together. Kit told Greg she didn't know. He asked her what time of year she used to go to the cottage where her uncle hurt her.

"In the summer."

Then he said, "It's summer, and you're packing." Suddenly Kit was crying a lot and shaking and curling up. "Is the Little Girl afraid now?" Greg asked. Kit nodded. "Is she wondering where she's going? Is she afraid you're taking her to her uncle?" Kit nodded again. "Can you tell her that you're not going there?" Kit did that.

Then she was remembering that when she was little she always packed a tiny suitcase when she went on a trip, especially when she went to the cottage. Little Kit put her special stuff in there, not socks or anything, but things like a shark's tooth and leaves. Big Kit reached in the suitcase and pulled out a shark's tooth and a eucalyptus leaf that smelled good. Then she picked up a paper person and a paper flower that her nieces made. Kit realized that Little Kit was doing what she always used to do, packing up her treasures, her portable home.

"And this time it's like her biggest fear come true," Greg added. "You're not just packing for the summer. You've lost your home. And your parents always told you—to reassure you—that if anything happened to them and you lost your home, you would be sent to your uncle and aunt."

Kit cried more. The young part of her that's called Little Kit was always afraid of losing her home and being sent to her uncle. That's what Little Kit thought was happening now. She was packing for the last time and getting ready to go live with her uncle forever. Kit cried a long time, all curled up on the floor. She told Little Kit that she wasn't going to her uncle's house and she asked Little Kit what she needed. "Don't ever leave me alone again. Don't forget me." Kit promised never to forget her again.

After a while Kit finished crying. She felt pretty good and she and Greg talked like grown-ups. "I'm so glad I let the young part of myself do what I needed," Kit said. "I've been struggling to separate the concept of home from this cabin. The young part of me did it. She can carry home with her in her suitcase. I've finally disconnected the concept from this place. I hadn't even seen the seam before."

Suddenly Kit was embarrassed about showing Greg her stuff. "There's a critical, disdainful voice telling me I was stupid to share my tawdry little objects with you. You're bored. You think I'm dumb."

Greg said, "I'm honored," and he reminded her that the critical voice waited longer than usual to interrupt when she was showing her real self to someone. Kit thought about that. It was true. That was good to notice.

During the days when Kit was moving her stuff from her cabin, she was thinking that she would probably want to do some kinda ceremony about leaving. She didn't know what it would be. She figured it would just happen if she let it. But the last day went by and all her stuff was gone, and she didn't do a ceremony. She worked all night the last night 'cause there wasn't any more time. After taking the last load over to Sarah's, she went back to the cabin and sat out back looking up the hill. First, it was just gray. Then more colors came out in the plants and rocks on the hillside.

One thing Kit thought about when she had to move was that she hadn't seen the fawns yet this year. She didn't want to go before seeing them. But you can't plan that sort of thing. So she was trying to get used to the idea of not seeing the fawns.

Before there was much color on the hill, Kit thought she heard a baby crying. Then she was sure she heard it. She stared at the hillside, but she couldn't see anything. The baby cried more. The sound moved to the right and then down and then a little to the left.

Kit knew what it was and she was trying to see the fawn. She had heard that sound before. Then she would see the mother deer run over to it and the crying would stop. Usually the fawn didn't cry too long 'cause the mother deer came pretty fast. But this fawn kept crying. Finally Kit could see it, wandering in a zig-zag along the hillside. It was just at the wild asparagus now. Kit liked to sit on the hill and eat the asparagus without picking it, you know, like a deer. Well, that's where the fawn was when Kit saw it. The hillside got pink and then yellow and then bright, almost like snow. The fawn kept crying and wandering through the cactus and the lupine and the grass beside the draw. Kit kept looking for the mother deer. Suddenly she yelled, "Mommy, where are you?" As soon as she heard her voice, she knew that the mommy wouldn't come. She was dead on a road, probably. She also knew that it was her, Little Kit, screaming for her mommy. At least her mommy wasn't dead on a road, but she was away when Little Kit needed her.

Big Kit sat there behind the cabin crying for a long time for the fawn which was sorta mixed up with Little Kit in her head.

So, the ceremony didn't happen, except that Kit saw the fawn.

A few days later it was the Fourth of July. That was the day three years ago when Kit first remembered about the bad stuff that happened. She called it her own Independence Day. Suddenly she thought, "Hey, maybe this is the day for the ritual leave-taking." She was all moved outa the cabin, but nobody else moved in yet. The whole day went by and Kit didn't get any idea about a ceremony. She went to a parade and had a picnic with friends until it rained. Then the rain stopped and they watched fireworks and then it was late and she started to drive to her friend's house in the mountains where she could sleep on the floor.

But then her car was on the dirt road near her cabin. She just sorta went there by accident, I guess. She picked up her concertina and the wicker suitcase—Little Kit kept it in the car these days—and walked up the path to her cabin, well, the cabin that used to be hers.

She stood out back and looked up at the hillside. It was a funny night for Colorado 'cause it felt wet. Thick clouds kept most of the moonlight away. Kit opened the suitcase and picked up each thing in it. She set them out on the little wooden deck. The bead necklace from Nat. The stones and leaves and seedpods. The picture of the Indian girl and the goat on the leaf. The stone bear in the pouch. A little candle. And everything else.

She played a sad tune on her concertina, the only tune she ever made up herself. She wasn't thinking about anything or making plans. She just let herself do whatever she wanted to do without asking why.

She lit the little candle and burnt some sage in the flame. Then she burnt the paper flower and the paper person from her nieces and the ashes stayed whole. It was a black flower and a black person, and suddenly they blew away into the darkness.

She picked up the candle, went into the cabin, and sat on the floor by the door. She could look south out the door, and up the hillside to the west out the long window. But she couldn't see much except when the clouds got thin for a few seconds. She just sat there and thought, "So, is this it? Am I done?" The candle kept burning. She looked at her watch. (She finally got a watch.) It was one minute till midnight. She looked out the window. She looked at the candle on the bare floor in the empty room. She looked out the door at a dark triangle against the dark sky. It was the rocks called the

Flatirons. She didn't feel any urge to do anything else. Just then, the candle burned out and the clouds separated, letting the bright moon shine on the hill and the draw where the fawns are born. "Hm." Kit smiled and then she laughed. "Too much."

She picked up the metal disk that was all that was left of the candle and went out back again. She threw the disk into the draw at the place where she found the dump from the people who lived in the cabin back in 1910. That's also where the mouse trap and the rock and the broken mouse skeleton were. She didn't know why she threw the disk in there. Probably nobody would ever find it, she told herself, 'cause she was feeling bad about littering. But, somehow, it didn't feel like littering. It felt more like putting something on an altar. She didn't know what it was. She didn't know what any of it was that she did that night. It was just her ceremony, her good bye.

22. Bread and Puppet

One of the places Kit went when she lost her cabin was her brother's house in Vermont. Nash and Mariel built the house themselves outa wood from an old barn that fell down and from trees they chopped down. It's a real good house with a high ceiling like a church and big windows looking out on a field that slopes down a big hill. If you keep looking that direction 'way out by the sky, you can see big mountains, not as high as in Colorado, but real pretty. The whole place where Nash and Mariel and their little girls live is real pretty.

Except the fields in front of the house, everything is forest there. Sweet-smelling balsam. And sugar maple that you can make sweet syrup from. And birch which tastes good if you chew the twigs. Come to think of it, they specialize in sweet trees. And snow. Lots of snow, so the easiest way to get down the hill from their house is on skis or a sled. But only in the winter, of course.

When Kit went there this time, it was summer and there were red raspberries and Queen Ann's lace instead of snow. Just as good, really, but you can't slide down the hill on them.

Nash and Mariel and their kids and some other people who live near there get together every Sunday morning just to sit quietly, and if you want to say something you can, but sometimes nobody says anything and they just sit there enjoying the quiet. They got the idea from Quakers. Kit was a little worried about going with them 'cause being on Sunday morning was sorta like church and she always felt sick in church. But she went and it wasn't like church. People just sat in chairs in a circle in the basement of the library. And they weren't dressed up like in church. Kit felt relaxed like she did in her big chair back at home... well, what used to be home.

Then a man said that he'd been thinking about Joseph Campbell and how he said it's important to "follow your bliss." And this man said he thought that was a bad thing and dangerous. It was going back to the idea of "do your own thing" and he thought that was selfish and irresponsible. Kit felt all hot in her chest and face. How could that guy say that? He must not understand what Campbell meant by bliss. He's not talking about running around being selfish and rude. He's talking about the same thing Quakers say about the inner light or "that of God in everyone." That man doesn't get it. But Kit was so angry, she couldn't think of anything to say. And this wasn't supposed to be a discussion or an argument. It was supposed to be like meditation and sharing. So, she didn't say anything, but she felt bad. Maybe she felt like that guy was talking about her, 'cause she was spending her life now following her instincts instead of thinking everything through and following a plan in her head. Maybe he was criticizing

her.
Another person said something a little later and then it was quiet again.

Near the end of the hour, a woman started talking calmly. She said that if a person never saw the sun but knew that it was a bright light, he might think a big light bulb was the sun the first time he saw it. But once he really did see the sun, he'd never make that mistake again. Once you see the sun, you would never think a light bulb was the sun again. After that, Kit felt relaxed and not angry anymore. That was the perfect thing to say. And it didn't have that angry flavor that Kit would have put in anything she said. But it said what she wanted to say: that there's a huge difference between selfishly doing your own thing, and opening to the real core of yourself and following your bliss.

On a farm on another hill a couple miles away lived some puppeteers. Every summer people from all over Vermont and all over the whole country and even from other countries like France and Siberia and—is Puerto Rico a different country?—all these people, maybe a hundred or two hundred, come to this farm in Vermont and put on a homemade circus. Some people live there all the time and make puppets as tall as a barn, that it takes three people or even more to work. One person might hold the pole for the body and somebody else holds the pole for a hand and like that. But if it's a dragon, there might be ten people inside a red cloth making a snaky dragon.

Anyway, besides the people who live there, all these other people come to work on the circus. Some of them come maybe two months early. People come whenever they can. Nash and Mariel and their two little girls, Reeve and•Kit, were gonna be in the show this summer. When Colorado Kit got there—they call her Colorado Kit to tell her apart from the other Kit—she went with them to the big field where they practiced for the circus.

She was real surprised to see so many people. And a lot of 'em were kids. She didn't know what she could do to help or if they needed her help, so she just stood in the field and watched a group of kids and one tall man working on a skit.

The man was the narrator and the kids were the actors. The man was kinda making up a crazy poem and the kids were acting it out. Then he'd stop and say, "Hm. OK. The family is real surprised. How about each person in the family say something you'd say when you're surprised." And each kid said something like Wow! or Gee whiz! The man didn't correct them or smile at them and say they were *ve*-ry *goo*-ood, the way grown-ups sometimes do and make you feel like you musta done something stupid. They were all working together, making up this skit. And it was good. And there was only one grown-up there and he liked the kids and their ideas and they all made it up together.

In one part, some of the kids put brown gunny sacks over themselves. They put one arm up into a corner of the sack where they had a cardboard beak stapled on. That arm was a long neck. Then they ran around saying, "Glue glue glue glue," real fast and they were turkeys. If you try saying that, you'll sound like a turkey, too.

Some of the kids made stilts with their parents and practiced walking on them. They tied them on their legs. Each of them had a big cardboard box around them. It hung by loops of twine from their shoulders. And each box had a cardboard horse head sticking out the front. And the kids had cardboard helmets. So they were knights on horses and they galloped around.

Kit got so interested in watching that she forgot to feel out of place. Then a woman in a brown skirt came through the field and said they needed people for the closing skit of the circus. Kit wasn't sure if she should volunteer since she was an outsider. She hadn't figured out yet that there aren't any outsiders there. But the brown woman came right up to her and handed her a song and said, "You're available, aren't you? You're not in the dancing bears act, are you? Here, let's go through the song once or twice." Kit didn't have a chance to explain to the lady that she didn't sing before they started practicing the song. Two other people came over and sang it with them. The brown lady asked what they'd like to be, cooks or TV news reporters or agricultural workers or child carers or whatever. She pointed to piles of clothes and props on the grass. There were gonna be a lota people in this skit. Kit saw a pot and an apron and she said she'd be a cook. The brown lady asked if she had a friend who could be another cook and Kit said yes. She could get Mariel to do it with her.

That night Colorado Kit looked at the song and tried to remember how it went, but she had trouble. Then she figured out how to play it on her concertina. Her fingers could remember better than her mouth. And Kit and Reeve could remember best of all. Pretty soon, everybody in the wooden house was singing the women workers' song. Mariel and Colorado Kit knew it perfectly by the time of the performance when they marched with all the other women into a big circle and did a sort of cooks' dance to the song while other people did the rice planters' dance or the seamstresses' dance or whatever. They couldn't see it, of course, but people in the audience said it looked real neat, all the different movements to the song.

Speaking of the audience, I heard a policeman say there were 20,000 people watching on Saturday. I don't know how many people were there on Sunday, but it looked the same to me. Nash and Mariel and the girls and Colorado Kit were all pretty surprised when they ran outa the woods into the field for the opening parade on Saturday, 'cause there were 20,000 people sitting around the curved hill watching all the stilt walkers and banners and streamers and kids and adults running outa the woods with the band playing.

Getting ready for the Bread and Puppet Circus—they call it *Bread* and Puppet 'cause they bake black bread all year and freeze it and then give it away to everyone who wants some—so, getting ready for the circus, Colorado Kit felt great. She liked how the kids were respected and there were no outsiders, anyone could join in. And she liked how they made everything outa cardboard and sheets and imagination. And she liked how *good* it was, even though it was homemade, and how funny some of the acts were and how sad some were and how much the audience loved it. She also liked how no one paid to come to see it and no one got paid.

23. Money

Money. Kit knew that was something she didn't have straightened out yet. There were a few big things that weren't straightened out. Lots of things were much better now that she knew the truth about her childhood, like her back and her stomach and no migraines. And so many things in her past made sense now, things that were mysteries before. Like why she always felt like such a bad person and why she was allergic to so many foods. Her body was afraid of so many things, especially things that someone said were good for it. And she knew why she hated baths and got sick in the shower and lurched and hit her head if someone knocked on the bathroom door. But there were still some things that weren't worked out yet, like money and men and trust. Probably others. But those were some that she was noticing.

Men was the one that bothered her the least. She figured she'd either start wanting to get a boyfriend or she wouldn't and she'd just see how that turned out.

Trust was a big one, though. Deep down inside, she still didn't have that feeling Georgia had, that she was safe and everything would turn out all right. Mostly, she just noticed that, though, like she did with the first sarcastic voice inside her head, and didn't try to push anything. She knew that the more she forced herself to do something 'cause it was good for her, the scareder she felt. So, she'd wait to see what happened with that one, too. And so far what happened was that if it got safe enough she would begin to trust someone. Like if it was for just a short time or just one specific way. Like, she trusted Greg to be a good therapist and respect her and not push her. And she trusted Dave not to be frightened of her memories. So, maybe it would gradually get better and she'd trust more people.

Then money. That was a tricky one, 'cause in the United States, as far as Kit knew, you need to have money and she didn't know how to get it. She called it "fitting into the cycling of resources" and she didn't know how to do it. She could hardly believe she used to earn money. Like other stuff, the harder she pushed herself to "get well and get productive" the weaker and crazier she felt.

After she became a Trager Practitioner, she still had trouble charging people for her work. So, mostly, she didn't. Sometimes people liked it a lot and gave her something afterward. One man fixed her broken table and broken chair. She liked that a lot. She knew people who paid her really liked what she did or they wouldn't have given her anything. If she made them pay, then she wouldn't be sure they really liked it. She knew there was something wrong with this way of doing things, but right then she couldn't do it another way. She thought she must be blocking the flow of money into her life, like a dammed river or a clogged artery. Greg asked her what she got out of doing that. His idea is that people aren't miserable for no reason. Well, if she didn't force people to give her money, then she knew that if they did give her some it was 'cause they wanted to. So, not charging money was a way of finding out that people liked her and thought what she did was good.

What else did she get from this way of living? If she didn't have money she didn't have to feel guilty about having more than she deserved. Also, she didn't have to be responsible for using it right and not wasting it. She didn't have to worry about losing it or being cheated. Once she started thinking about it, Kit realized there were lots of things she got from not earning money.

Greg helped her think about other ways she could get those benefits that wouldn't keep money from coming to her. He also reminded her that things are usually like a dimmer switch and not like an on/off switch. It might not be bright, but it might not be completely dark. Gradually Kit started getting paid for a few things she did. It was a real gradual dimmer switch, and she still doesn't have this stuff all worked out, but it's getting easier.

24. Wet Suit

A couple years back, Georgia told Kit about an experiment with breast cancer patients. The ones who could tell the story of how it turned out OK mostly got better and didn't die. "So, I should write such a story," Kit was thinking. She didn't know yet if she had breast cancer, but the doctors seemed in a big hurry to schedule the biopsy for tomorrow.

But when she sat down to write, she couldn't do it. She was thinking that was a bad sign, not even to be able to *start* the story of how it turned out OK. Actually, there was a different story pushing to come out, the one about how it turned out awful. Writing that story felt like condemning herself to death, but she finally gave herself permission to do it. More and more, she was letting herself do what her insides were pushing to do, even if it didn't seem sensible. After all, it wasn't sensible for Joseph to leave his good job in Los Angeles and eat garbage. Here's the story:

> So, she had the biopsy and it was cancer and she knew she was going to die. And she started thinking about what she wanted to do before she died. And she realized that what she really wanted to do was to let in the love that surrounded her. Suddenly she knew that although she couldn't feel that love, she was living and always had lived in an ocean of warmth and love, but she was insulated from it by something like a psychic wet suit. And she spent the rest of her days gradually peeling back pieces of that wet suit and letting the warmth touch her and being part of the ocean. Dying was no big deal after that. Everyone does it. The point isn't to avoid dying but to have lived before you die.

Kit was thinking that wasn't hard and it didn't even turn out awful. "By giving myself permission to write the story of how it turned out horribly, I was able to drain off the sludge that was blocking the story of how it turned out OK." She decided to write another story.

> She has the biopsy and it's cancer and she faces the possibility of death and notices the wet suit and learns to become part of the flow of love and then doesn't die of the disease after all but lives to be an old woman. And all the time, she's aware of the ocean of

> love that we're all floating in, all part of. And that awareness was infectious, so that everywhere she went she found a circle of warmth which continued to spread even when she wasn't there.

Things were rolling now. She wrote another.

> This is the story about how it turns out not to be cancer but she learns the lesson about love anyway. She was so thrilled and relieved that she didn't have cancer and had brushed so closely to the other possiblities that she started to live her life as if she had come back from death. Magic was no longer occasional but constant. She learned to slide down the rockslide with grace and without effort, enjoying the dance between solidity and fluidity. Without being planned, the most wonderful things were always there. And she learned not to worry about finding love, that she carried it with her and was floating in it and would never be without it.

Shoot, she was going to write how it turned out horrible and she ended up writing three stories about how it turned out great. She knew all along that it was a matter of life and death. But now she knew that it didn't matter what happened at the biopsy. The point wasn't whether she died next month of cancer but whether she lived before she died, whenever that was.

Kit lay in her Mexican hammock and watched the aspen leaves flash yellow and green. Her eyes closed. Then all us kids got in the hammock with her, Little Kit and me and the

Orphan. We wanted to know about the operation. Kit said it would be the next day and that a small piece of her breast would be cut out by a woman who knew how to do that very carefully. She would give Kit a shot so it wouldn't hurt. Then Kit told us that we didn't have to go. We could play in the mountain cabin where she was staying for a few weeks or we could sleep in the hammock or follow the creek up through the aspen to the meadow or... Suddenly she realized that we didn't need her suggestions. We would do what we wanted and have a good time. I'm magic, after all, and I'd invent all kindsa interesting things to play with, just like I always did.

Kit called up a friend of hers to see if the folkdancers were going to the Brazilian dance that night. He said they were. Even though Kit didn't know any dances from Brazil she danced like crazy, jumping and twirling all around when the drums played real loud and wild.

Kit danced with her friend Chris for a while. They danced so close that Kit didn't even have to think about how to follow his leads; his body just moved hers. It was a dream come true for Kit. She always thought how neat that would be, how relaxing, if it was possible, which she didn't think it would be. But now she found out it was possible, and even more fun than she imagined.

Then another friend started dancing with Kit and Chris. They made up lots of stuff, tossing each other from one to the other, spinning a tight ring with a buzz step, one person falling against the other two. Suddenly Kit went up in the air with the two guys' arms swooping under her like a swing. Then the men used their arms like a slingshot and threw her up and out into the middle of the dance floor. Sometimes, they did something so silly that they'd all start laughing and even strangers were laughing.

After a while, Kit danced with another friend. He tried to "pick up some women" but they weren't interested, so he asked Kit to dance. Kit didn't mind. She knew he was a little crazy about women and maybe a little crazy in general, but nice and a lot of fun. He invented lots of dance things. Not everything worked, but because he was willing to experiment right at the edge of being out of control, he discovered some really exciting ways to move. He lifted Kit into the air in more ways than she thought were possible, including using his thigh. They twisted, leaned, dipped low, sailed high, flew apart, and oozed together. For some reason, Kit didn't get embarrassed, even when an experiment threw them into an awkward position or dropped her on the floor. And when other people were laughing, she was laughing, too. It was loads of fun.

After that, Kit danced a lot more with Chris. She liked his soft, close moving after the other guy's wild dancing, which she also liked. Chris's experiments were fun, too, and real easy to follow. And she liked that Chris obviously liked dancing with her. She wasn't just any woman.

Kit was thinking that dancing helped her dip into the pool of love that's... gee, she didn't know whether to say "inside me" or "all around me." It felt like both, or neither, or there wasn't any difference. And it didn't have anything to do with "falling" in love or even with specific people. It was just something that was always there. It wasn't so much that dancing took her to the spring as that it helped her stop blocking the flow from it. "This spring has been here all along. And I've been here—exerting enormous amounts of effort to keep myself dry. What a pleasure to relax and bathe in the water."

Then Kit went back to the cabin in the mountains. When she went to bed she was thinking, "I'm going to dance a lot more before I die."

Back before all this happened, before she remembered her

childhood, Kit met an old man by the Rio Grande. He just got outa a mental hospital. They walked by the river together and talked about birds and being crazy or not being crazy and about children and parents and religion. And suddenly, while they were in the middle of a thicket of thorns, he turned toward Kit and shouted, "FEAR... is the opposite of love." Kit was scared 'cause he moved so sharply and she was caught in a sticker bush. She thought it was a big mistake to go walking with the old man. But then he turned back around and kept walking. After a minute he explained, "People think that hate is the opposite of love, but it isn't. Fear is the opposite of love. Love isn't something you have to look for or learn. It's what people experience naturally unless it's blocked by fear. You don't need to learn how to love. You need to unblock it by letting out the fear."

Nowadays, Kit thought a lot about that man.

25. Surgery

At the last minute, I decided to go with Kit when she had her operation. I thought she might need me, and I was right. The nurse was real nice. She knew about Kit's bad memories and she knew that the operation might bring back some of the old feelings. She played relaxing music on a tape player that she borrowed from her son. And she let Kit bring her friend Dave and me. Well, I don't think she knew I was there, but I'm sure it was all right. Dave was a good person to have there 'cause he knew about Kit's memories and he understood them 'cause he had memories like that, too.

Kit got stiff and started drifting away as soon as she lay down and the doctor bent Kit's arm back over her head. Dave said, "It's OK. That's the surgeon. You're uncle isn't here. There's no one here but the doctor, the nurse and me. No one else. And it's OK."

They put a shot of something into Kit's breast and the doctor cut her. She steadied her cutting hand on Kit's chest. Kit stopped breathing. She thought something heavy was crushing her. I quick told her I was there, too. She seemed real glad. I heard the doctor ask Kit if she could feel anything. But Kit couldn't talk or move or anything. The surgeon kept asking her if she could feel it. I saw Kit's face curl up. And the hand that was holding Dave's hand got real tight. Suddenly Dave said, "I'm sure she's feeling it. She just can't talk." They gave her another shot.

Kit and I started swinging in the air swing. But she kept looking down and seeing the doctor leaning on her chest. After the operation, the nurse said, "I wish I knew where you went."

Kit said, "No you don't. I mean, you wouldn't want to go there." I don't think she was talking about the swing. I think she was talking about the way she couldn't breathe when the surgeon steadied her hand on her chest and the way she couldn't talk even when she felt the cutting and the burning.

The day after the operation, Kit thought of a weird thing. For two years she'd been trying to convince her parents that cutting Uncle Ned outa the family was not going to fix everything. She said she thought the whole family had a sickness and cutting off one part wouldn't cure it. Like cutting off the rash wouldn't cure you of smallpox. She said they all had their parts in the disease. It wasn't one person's problem but everyone's. A whole body gets smallpox, not just the skin.

But when Kit found out that something was growing inside her, she thought, "I know this feeling. Something bad and ugly is invading my body, and I'm helpless to stop it." After the operation she thought, "That feels great. I was wrong. At least symbolically, surgical removal of the invader feels wonderful."

Later that day she changed her mind. "The ugly bad thing

invading my body all my life wasn't my uncle. It was the shame I felt about what happened. That's what the surgeon helped me remove."

Seemed like each time Kit found a way to act out getting clean—like in the river in the redwood forest or with the operation—she felt better.

The woman asked Kit why she was cutting wood so soon after her operation. "You could get someone else to do that," she said.

"But I want to do it. It feels good. I don't know if I can explain this, but until a few days ago I thought I had cancer. I was thinking a lot about death. Now that I know I don't have cancer, that I'm not about to die, suddenly I want to do everything. I want to cut the wood and cook the soup and climb the mountain and dance the dance. I want to live my life, not just do my time."

Part VI

OUTSIDE TIME: DESERT HEART
(1990, Kit)

So walk I on uplands unbounded
And know that there is hope
For that which thou didst mold out of dust
To have consort with things eternal.

Dead Sea Scrolls

The earth will give you food.
The river will give you water.
This woman will have your child.
The earth will be your grave.
But the dance winds on.
So dance now: don't cry.

Old Swedish song

The rock fit against my body perfectly. Or, rather, my body fit against the rock. It was warm, rounded, a bit coarse, but not rough. This coarseness was important, a sign of maturity, like the difference between an adult's skin and a child's. This was a mature rock. My tears made dark stains on it.

Here was the moment I'd been moving toward, without knowing it, all day. No, for two days. Actually, I'd known for months that I had something to do in the Utah desert. Something. I didn't know what. I'd planned a backpacking trip for October, but ended up having minor surgery instead. That was important, too. I pulled off my shirt and, aware of the scar on my left breast, pressed my skin against the red rock.

All day, I'd been walking through a feminine landscape, rounded, curved, folded. Now I cupped my body against one of those round forms.

For the past half hour, I'd been aware of a building urge to do this, to press my surface against the surface of this warm, feminine sandstone. But the sun was below the canyon rim, the rocks looked cold now, and I needed to reach the car and go pick up my friends who were walking out through a different canyon.

Then, coming around a point, I turned suddenly into the pink sunlight and rolled ever-so-slowly, because I knew at once that this was the rock, against the maternal shape.

But that's not the point—which rock or even what time. It

was the confluence of stone, sun, my day's journey, my life's path, and who knows what other mysteries. There'd be no point in my returning to that stone or in sending someone else there. The crossing of threads, the convergence of all those elements is past. Now there's just a chunk of sandstone there. And tomorrow at sunset, I will be a different person from the one who hugged the stone in the pink sun today. I fantasized briefly about a religious cult forming around the stone, building an altar by it and then a temple over it. How many times had I done that, keying on a concrete object associated with a spiritual awakening and missing the point of the experience itself and the lesson that each of us can be open to our own?

But today, my life and my body were touched by a mothering landscape. "Mommy," I heard myself say as I eased my weight against the stone. A few hours later, it occurred to me that the scale of the rock to me was the same as my mother to me as a child. The tears came before I made contact. First hands and arms, then thighs, belly, chest, and cheek gave in to the rock. The late afternoon sun warmed my back and the stone my front. I felt held between two large, warm hands.

Suddenly, a burst of warmth entered my solar plexus as if from the rock. It was alive and wonderful. Before I could fully form the question, the answer was clear.

My heart.

With a steadiness that surprised me, I pushed away from the stone. First there was a petroglyph of a woman's head with three loops hanging from one ear and two from the other—my shadow, one loop of my earring having been lost.

Already, I was discounting the experience. "You just made it up about your heart," a reasonable voice reminded me.

"Sure, but that doesn't diminish its significance," another voice offered.

As I increased the distance between me and the rock, I took

a quick breath for there, centered in the chest of my shadow, was a hole the size of my fist, with a flared rim, as if something had exploded from inside the stone. For the skeptic in me, the scar. "Too much." I smiled.

The river and the sweat lodge had taken my heart from me for safety on the trip. Where had I heard those words? That's what Amos had said "We'd like to offer you a sweat for safety on your trip." At the time, I'd thought only of the ten-day canoe trip, not the several-year exploration that I had no idea I was about to begin. Now, the desert, the earth, my mother, had restored my heart to me, when I was strong enough both to protect it and to receive its gifts.

As I put on my shirt and continued walking, thoughts, memories, scraps of song moved with me across the slickrock.

I want to sleep with you in the desert tonight.

I was singing to myself. On the canyon floor came the words:

I learned a long time ago
What a man can do to your soul.

He came close to destroying it, I thought, the way you might unintentionally squash a spider as you thrashed with a fever. But he didn't. I'm still here and more alive everyday.

I got a peaceful, easy feelin'.
I know you won't let me down...

My hand gripped a rock above me and prepared to pull my weight up to the canyon rim. I looked at my hand and sang that line again.

I got a peaceful, easy feelin'.
I know you won't let me down...

My hand, my self would not let me down.

Another Kate Wolf song floated by, "The Trumpet Vine." The same line that always makes me cry did it again.

You came when you were needed.

I thought of the rock.

I could not ask for more
Than to turn and see you walkin'
Through the kitchen door.

I thought of the glow of my mother in "the kitchen in my mind" and of the maternal glow of the rock and of Toby standing in the half-opened screen door at the cottage.

The vegetation had changed, and the rocks. I turned to say good-bye to the magic landscape, but it was already gone. That seemed fine. I didn't have to think of some significant leave-taking. Something happened. It was over. And I walked on, changed by it. Later, when I was suddenly back on slickrock, I was able to enjoy the reprise without the weight of having to do something profound.

THE END